SCHOOL LIBRARY MEDIA SERIES

Edited by Diane de Cordova Biesel

1. *Chalk Talk Stories*, written and illustrated by Arden Druce, 1993.
2. *Toddler Storytime Programs*, by Diane Briggs, 1993.
3. *Alphabet: A Handbook of ABC Books and Book Extensions for the Elementary Classroom, second edition*, by Patricia L. Roberts, 1994.
4. *Cultural Cobblestones: Teaching Cultural Diversity*, by Lynda Miller, Theresa Steinlage, and Mike Printz, 1994.
5. *ABC Books and Activities: From Preschool to High School*, by Cathie Hilterbran Cooper, 1996.
6. *ZOOLUTIONS: A Mathematical Expedition with Topics for Grades 4 through 8,* by Anne Burgunder and Vaunda Nelson, 1996.
7. Library Lessons for Grades 7–9, by Arden Druce, 1997.
8. *Counting Your Way through 1–2–3 Books and Activities,* by Cathie Hilterbran Cooper, 1997.
9. *Art and Children: Using Literature to Expand Creativity,* by Robin W. Davis, 1996.
10. *Story Programs: A Source Book of Materials, second edition,* by Carolyn Sue Peterson and Ann Fenton, 1998.
11. *Taking Humor Seriously in Children's Literature: Literature-*Based Mini-Units and Humorous Books for Children Ages 5–12, by Patricia L. Roberts, 1997.
12. Multicultural Friendship Stories and Activities for Children, Ages 5–14, by Patricia L. Roberts, 1997.
13. *Side by Side: Twelve Multicultural Puppet Plays,* by Jean M Pollock, 1997.
14. *Reading Fun: Quick and Easy Activities for the Media Center,* by Mona Kerby, 1997.
15. Paper Bag Puppets, by Arden Druce with illustra aldine Hulbert, Cynthia Johnson, Harvey H. Live_____ _____ Ditter Waters, 1998.
16. *Once Upon a Childhood: Fingerplays, Action Rhymes, and Fun Times for the Very Young*, Dolores C. Chupela, 1998.
17. *Bulletin Bored? or Bulletin Boards!: K–12*, Patricia Sivak and Mary Anne Passatore, 1998.
18. *Color and Shape Books for All Ages,* Cathie Hilterbran Cooper, 1998.

Bulletin Bored?
or
Bulletin Boards!

K-12

Patricia Sivak

and

Mary Anne Passatore

Illustrated by Mary Anne Passatore

School Library Media Series, No. 17

The Scarecrow Press, Inc.
Lanham, Maryland, & London
1998

SCARECROW PRESS, INC.

Published in the United States of America
by Scarecrow Press, Inc.
4720 Boston Way
Lanham, Maryland 20706

4 Pleydell Gardens, Folkestone
Kent CT20 2DN, England

British Library Cataloguing in Publication Information Available

Library of Congress Cataloging-in-Publication Data

Sivak, Patricia, 1949-
    Bulletin bored? or bulletin boards! : K-12 / Patricia Sivak and
Mary Anne Passatore ; illustrated by Mary Anne Passatore.
        p.   cm. — (School library media series ; no. 17)
    Includes bibliographical references.
    ISBN 0-8108-3538-X (paper : alk. paper)
    1. Bulletin boards.   I. Passatore, Mary Anne, 1943- .
II. Title.   III. Series.
LB 1043.58.S58 1998   98-27586
371.33'56—dc21   CIP

In memory of Doctor Margaret (Peggy) Grote
who encouraged me to pursue my dream
of writing this book.

In honor of my mother Mildred Sivak who
gave me the time to be creative.

—*Patricia Sivak*

In dedication to my husband, James Passatore,
whose encouragement, support, and creative contributions provided me
with the time and inspiration essential to
the completion of this book.

—*Mary Anne Passatore*

CONTENTS

CONTENTS

CONTENTS

CONTENTS

EDITOR'S FOREWORD

The School Library Media Series is directed to the school library media specialist, particularly the building-level librarian. The multifaceted role of the librarian as educator, collection developer, curriculum developer, and information specialist is examined. The series includes concise, practical books on topical and current subjects related to programs and services.

In themes ranging from thought provoking to fanciful, Patricia Sivak and Mary Anne Passatore have provided educators, librarians, and care givers with a collection of designs for bulletin boards. The directions are simple and clear; the artwork is refreshing; and an interesting system for cutting block letters is offered.

The busy adult who works with children and young people will find many useful and practical ideas in this book.

—Diane de Cordova Biesel
Series Editor

AUTHORS' NOTE

When we—a school librarian and an art teacher—discovered that we had a common love of, and knack for doing, bulletin boards, we joked about how "someday" we would share our ideas by writing a book.

This desire to share—a teacher's greatest satisfaction—was so strong that we decided not to wait for "someday." Thus, *Bulletin Bored? or Bulletin Boards!* was born.

Pat, as a junior high librarian, has always enjoyed filling her library with colorful, seasonal, theme-related bulletin boards. Her visual inspirations come from varied sources, including greeting cards, magazine advertisements, book catalogs, and even cocktail napkins. The slogans can be book or song titles, popular expressions, catchy rhymes, or school-spirited sayings.

Some of Pat's efficient time-savers include: keeping the best of displays, laminating them when possible, creating a bulletin board archives that is organized by season, and sometimes recycling an "oldie." She also assigns student assistants as library artists, and she always photographs finished bulletin boards, filing the photos in a constantly growing resource notebook.

Mary Anne, with thirty years' experience in art education spanning first grade through twelfth grade, has also done her share of bulletin board displays. Her ideas have been designed to fit make-do locations around or on windows and doors, to full-stage and gymnasium exhibits. Mary Anne gladly shares her "tricks of the trade" ranging from versatile hand-crafted, hinged characters to stencil-free block lettering. All of the art in this book is unique, adaptable, and easy to reproduce.

We have combined Pat's bulletin board ideas with Mary Anne's originality to create this book. *Bulletin Bored? or Bulletin Boards!* is filled with classroom-tested displays that anyone—teacher, librarian, club sponsor, secretary, and so on—can use. Let our art, slogans, and ideas spark your own creativity!

TO USE THIS BOOK

The bulletin board ideas are located in chronological order following the school year from September to June. In addition, you'll find ideas for sports, the arts, popular and controversial topics, careers, summer fun, and more. There are pages of patterns, "how-to's," and lots of helpful hints.

All art is original and can be easily reproduced or enlarged. Many designs are cross-referenced and can be recycled for a different season, subject, or event. The art appears on the right side with corresponding directions, slogans, and additional ideas on the left.

For extra help and information, we have included a glossary of terms, a listing of types of companies and suppliers that donate their scraps, overruns, and discards to schools and clubs, and special effects.

OVERHEAD PROJECTOR

Choose a pattern from the book. Enlarge the pattern by using an overhead projector and the following steps:

1. Using a permanent marker or an overhead pen, trace the pattern on a clear sheet of acetate, a plastic bag, or wax paper. If you have a thermofax machine available, place copy and acetate sheet in the machine to make a copy.
2. Choose appropriate sized paper and tape to a wall.
3. Place the acetate sheet on the overhead projector and project the picture onto the paper.
4. Move the projector forward to make the picture smaller or move it backward to enlarge the picture.
5. Trace the projected image.

If a copying machine is available with the capability to enlarge or reduce, patterns can be appropriately sized.

HELPFUL HINTS

As you walk the flea markets, go to garage sales, or shop discount stores that specialize in close-outs, keep your eyes open for props that could be used for a bulletin board. For example, a paper Christmas fireplace as tall as a bulletin board and with small stockings is very effective. Sometimes explaining how the item will be used persuades people to donate the material.

Since three-dimensional items are often attractive and eye-catching, some useful pieces are:

- denim shorts/jeans
- plastic or silk flowers
- styrofoam sheets (use a saber saw or electric carving knife for cutting)
- pom-poms, buttons, trim, ribbon, lace, doilies
- fake fur, fabrics, felt
- plastic white garbage bags (great ghosts)
- plastic black garbage bags (witches or bats)
- articles of clothing (for skeleton, snowman, little boy or girl)
- heavy white cord, twine, rope, yarn, kite string

OTHER HELPFUL HINTS

- Artcraft paper does not fade. It comes in various sizes and can be used over and over again. Another fade-resistant background is a colored plastic tablecloth.
- Wrapping paper has beautiful designs that can often correspond with subject matter.
- Magazine covers and pages, junk mail, and brochures provide patterns and textural colors.
- Black and white can be used for backgrounds and left up for the entire year. For the best visibility and contrast, use the black background as often as possible and staple white or other colors over it.
- All bulletin board materials should be laminated for protection and lasting color. If no laminator is available, use clear contact paper.
- Use large art portfolios or make storage containers from oversized cardboard, poster or matte boards, and organize by season, month, or subject.
- After a major holiday, pick up materials on sale for next year's decorations.
- Book jackets can be added to any bulletin board or books can be placed on a separate table below or near the display.

Welcome a-board! We're loaded with ideas (see pp. 6–7).

Here's the support; you provide the direction. (See pp. 10–11)

BACK-TO-SCHOOL
Welcome Letters

SPECIAL EFFECTS

Lettering

- Construction paper, poster board, foamcore, cardboard, fabric, contact paper, school book covers, magazine pages, photographs, newspaper/comic strips, recycled paper, wrapping paper, wallpaper
- See **Lettering "How-To's"** (pp. 220–29)

Eyes

- Construction paper, felt, poster board, fabrics
- Three-dimensional effect—margarine lids, aerosol can lids, ping pong balls
- Plastic moving eyes for smaller letters

Smiles/Arms/Legs

- Construction paper, poster board, felt, fabric, pipe cleaners, yarn, macrame cord, actual clothing such as mittens, hats, scarves, ear muffs

Accessories

- Actual objects such as party hats, noise makers, balloons, confetti, small wrapped packages

- Construction paper, wrapping paper, contact paper, shelf paper, wallpaper

COLOR SUGGESTIONS

- Use school colors or seasonal colors

ADDITIONAL IDEAS

- Arms hold school supplies, student papers, photographs, book jackets, etc.
- Lettering cut from recycled paper such as old tests, book reports, students' work, etc.

SUGGESTED USES

- Welcome lettering—opening of school, Open House, guest speakers, parent conferences, Career Day
- Birthday lettering—student and faculty birthdays, historical birthdays, literature birthdays
- School spirit lettering—pep Club, cheerleading, band, or any school activity

BACK-TO-SCHOOL
School Supplies

SPECIAL EFFECTS

Supplies

- Construction paper, poster board, aluminum foil, clear plastic, lightweight wood, woodgrain contact paper
- Display space—poster board, corkboard, plywood

COLOR SUGGESTIONS

- Actual colors
- School colors
- Primary colors—red/blue/yellow

ADDITIONAL IDEAS

Border

- Surround windows, bulletin boards, doorways, chalkboards, teacher's desks, storage cabinets, etc.

School supplies

- Reduce size of school supplies and place in the hands of "Welcome" letters

Actual school supplies

- Arrange in a lunch box
- Paste on poster board
- Substitute school supplies for other classroom materials such as book jackets, sheet music, shop tools, test tubes

Display space

- Use for slogan, message, or school projects

SUGGESTED USES

- Announcement
- Message Board
- Open House
- Curriculum
- Library/Office/Cafeteria
- Church Activities
- Clubs/Organizations

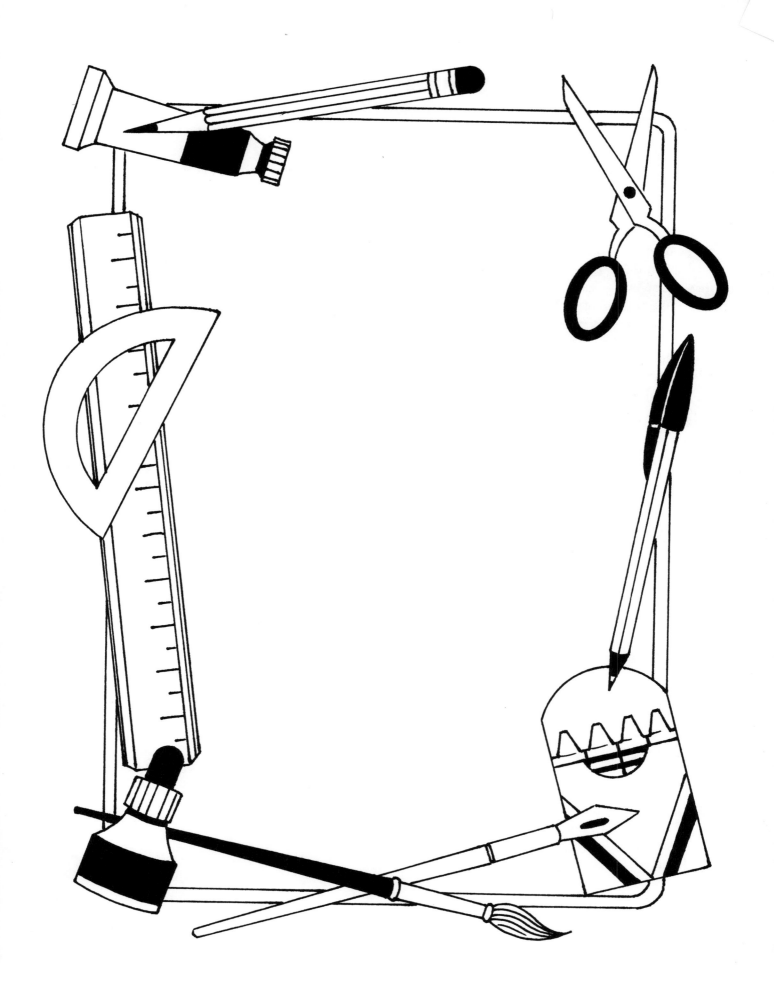

BACK-TO-SCHOOL
School "Kids"

SPECIAL EFFECTS

Body

- Construction paper, poster board, foamcore, fabric, upson board, plywood, gift box cardboard
- Use brass fasteners for movable joints with the following lightweight materials: paper, foamcore, or poster board
- Use bolts to fasten joints with the following heavier materials: plywood and upson board
- Paint brass fastener or bolt heads to blend with skin tones and clothing

Face/Arms/Legs

- Construction paper, poster board, foamcore, kraft paper

Clothing

- Construction paper, poster board, wallpaper, wrapping paper, fabric
- Dress figures with actual clothing

Hair

- Yarn, fun fur, rope, felt, fabric, rubber matting

COLOR SUGGESTIONS

- Body—peach, brown, tan, yellow, red, black
- Hair—yellow, red, brown, black

SLOGANS

- Welcome to the Bunch
- Two Can Work Together
- Your Best Foot Forward (for grooming or fashion)
- This Is the Year of the Reader
- We Can't Have Success Without You
- Welcome Back to Reading
- We Are E.T. (Extra Terrific)
- Look Who's Back for More Reading
- A New Scoop of Kids (holding an ice cream cone)
- This School Has Class!

ADDITIONAL IDEAS

Clothing and accessories

- Vary for any season
- Can represent a cultural or ethnic event
- Extracurricular activities—clubs, cheerleading, sports, band, etc.
- Curricular activities—jogging outfit for exercise, apron for home economics or shop class, hats for careers

"Kids"

- Use alone or in groups, vary the size, personalize, make freestanding or stationary and unhinged
- Arm and leg patterns can be reversed
- Use any of our "kids" for a variety of faces, hairstyles, body positions and clothing

SUGGESTED USES

- Career Day—See **Patterns** (pp. 186–219)
- Library/Office/Cafeteria
- Clubs/Organizations
- Curriculum—"kids" can hold school materials
- Church activities

BACK-TO-SCHOOL
Signpost

SPECIAL EFFECTS

Freestanding sign

- Set in basket filled with sand, gravel, or plaster
- Set post in hole of cinder block

Post

- Cardboard, foamcore, poster board, yardstick, 1" x 3" firring strip, 2 x 4 wood
- For weathered look, lightly brush or sponge the post with watered-down paint

Post base

- Natural or synthetic flowers, cut paper or cardboard, clear plastics, foils, cotton batting

Bucket

- Decorate with seasonal art, ribbons, stickers, borders, or woodgrain contact paper
- Cover with burlap, seasonal fabric, or wrapping paper
- Tie with string, rope, ribbon, raffia, etc.

Signs

- Poster board, heavy brown cardboard, foamcore, construction paper

SLOGANS

- On the Way to Research
- Try These!
- Point Me in the Right Direction
- Show Me the Way
- Signs of the Time
- Directions to Success

ADDITIONAL IDEAS

Post

- Use existing classroom pole/pillar

Freestanding sign

- Use as a directional sign in classroom, hallway, cafeteria, office, or outside

Research in the library

- Use signpost for words such as: Books, Computers, Encyclopedias, Magazines

Seasonal

- Decorate base of post

SUGGESTED USES

- Curriculum
- Classroom/Room/Teacher's name
- Goals for the year
- Course outline or unit
- Library/Office/Cafeteria
- Clubs/Organizations
- Church Activities

BACK-TO-SCHOOL
Owl/Blackboard

SPECIAL EFFECTS

Owl

- Construction paper, poster board, kraft paper, fun fur, corrugated cardboard, felt

Eyes

- Plastic moving eyes, felt, Ping-Pong balls, aerosol can lids

Hat

- Drapery tie back for tassel, actual school tassel

Chalk/Eraser

- Felt, poster board
- Three-dimensional effect:
  Small box covered in felt
  White drinking straws

COLOR SUGGESTIONS

- Owls—brown, black, gray, tan, white, school colors
- Chalkboard—green, black, white

SLOGANS

- Be Wise! Read!

- Look Whoooooooo's Back
- Chalk Up These Ideas
- Look Whooooooo's Reading
- What's New (use to point)
- "Owl" Be Glad to Show You How

ADDITIONAL IDEAS

Owl

- Remove cap and use for Halloween
- Place school pennant/flag on wing
- Display slogan or message on body

Frame

- Use alone as a border

Chalkboard

- Use actual or existing classroom chalkboard or window
- Actual eraser and chalk

SUGGESTED USES

- Seasonal
- Curriculum
- Library/Office/Cafeteria
- Open House
- Church Activities

BACK-TO-SCHOOL
Houses

SPECIAL EFFECTS

Schoolhouse

- Construction paper, poster board, kraft paper, foamcore

Haunted house

- Construction paper, poster board, kraft paper, foamcore
- For weathered look, lightly brush or sponge the siding with watered-down gray or white paint

COLOR SUGGESTIONS

Schoolhouse

- Building—red, ivory, gray, light blue
- Windows—yellow, manila, white
- Roof—brown, black
- Bell—yellow/gold with brown, red or black interior

Haunted house

- Same as schoolhouse

SLOGANS

Schoolhouse

- "Every School's a Good School"
- School's Out
- Dear Teachers/Students. Welcome Back!
- Another Opening, Another Year

Haunted house

- The Best Little Horror House
- Read a Haunting Book
- It's Haunting!

ADDITIONAL IDEAS

Schoolhouse

- Omit half-round window above door. Substitute with sign or banner lettered "School," "Open House," "Welcome," "American Education Week," or the name of your school
- Cut out door, windows, and bell tower and back with brightly colored construction paper
- Add "kids" (see pp. 6–9)
- Simplify design by outlining and cutting a silhouette

Haunted house

- Recycle schoolhouse as a haunted house
- Remove bell and flag
- Change door and window openings to black paper
- Add a few tilted, unhinged, shutters
- Extra scary objects can be added such as: spook eyes, spider webs, ghosts, bats, pumpkins, witches, mummies, full moon, or fence

CURRICULUM USES

- Curriculum
- Seasonal, especially Halloween
- American Education Week
- Welcome or Open House
- End of the School Year
- Library/Office/Cafeteria
- Clubs/Organizations
- Church Activities

HALLOWEEN
Pumpkins

SPECIAL EFFECTS

Pumpkins

- Construction paper, foamcore, poster board, fabrics, magazine pages/covers, wrapping paper, wallpaper

COLOR SUGGESTIONS

- Pumpkins—orange, yellow-orange, red-orange, tans, browns, yellows
- Stems/Tops/Grass—greens, yellows, browns, tan
- Lettering—white, yellow, orange, brown, black, neon orange, green

SLOGANS

- Can You Top This? (art, music, literature)
- It's a Howl!
- Pumpkin Patch Poems (book reports, essays, etc.
- Grisly Giggles
- Chilling Chuckles

ADDITIONAL IDEAS

Faces

- Paint or outline with magic markers
- Cut out facial features and back with black paper, written words, or photo montage
- Omit faces—use large pumpkins as display areas for student works, instructional needs, announcements, etc.

Pumpkins

- Stack according to space available: group (a pumpkin patch), spread out horizontally as a border, stack in a pyramid, use as peek-overs. Arrange vertically as a totem pole on any space that is tall and narrow (great on or next to a door or pillar)
- Use individual pumpkins as a name tags

Letters

- See **Lettering "How-To's"** (pp. 220–29) Make mouth a large silhouette letter

SUGGESTED USES

- Seasonal
- Curriculum
- Library/Office/Cafeteria
- Clubs/Organizations
- Church Activities

HAPPY
HALLOWEEN

HALLOWEEN
Witches

SPECIAL EFFECTS

Witch's cloak

- Construction paper, foamcore, poster board, fabric

Moon

- Corrugated cardboard, foamcore, burlap, glossy fabric such as silk, satin, lining

Hair

- Yarn, corn husks, raffia, paper ribbon

Broom

- Actual broom, corn husks, straw, or broom bristles glued to cardboard form

Handle

- Dowel rod

COLOR SUGGESTIONS

- Face—yellow, orange, lime green
- Hat—black
- Letters—school colors, black/orange, yellow, brown, neon colors
- Silhouette—black on circle of orange, yellow, or white
- Hair—black, white, gray

SLOGANS

- Look What's Brewing at the . . . (Library, Classroom, Gym, Game)
- A Web of Suspense (mysteries)
- We Know Witch's the Best Team Around
- Spooktacular Books (Reports, Art, etc.)

- Brew Up a Victory
- Bat the . . . (opponent)
- Be-Witching Ideas
- Brew Up Success
- We're Brewing Up a Victory
- "Witch" Is Correct

ADDITIONAL IDEAS

Witch's cloak

- Staple dark fabric under face and drape into folds
- Use choir robe or graduation gown

Witch

- Hold student works or curriculum-related materials
- Use as a peekover

Sports team logos

- Add to cloak or hat

Cauldron

- Add and fill with student materials, reports, etc.
- See **Spring** (pp. 68–89)

Letters

- See **Lettering "How-To's"** (pp. 220–20)

SUGGESTED USES

- Curriculum
- Library/Office/Cafeteria
- School Spirit Week
- Clubs/Organizations

These versatile squashes can be September's harvest, October's Jack-o-lanterns, and November's thanksgiving pies. Recycle your pumpkins (see pp. 16–17).

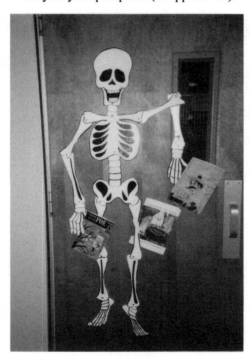

"The 'head bone's' connected to the 'Halloween-bone'; 'the Halloween bone's' connected to the 'school spirit bone'; 'the school spirit bone's' connected to the 'Phys Ed Bone'; Now here's the way to a board!" (See pp. 24–26.)

HALLOWEEN
Ghosts

SPECIAL EFFECTS

Body

- Construction paper, poster board, foamcore, fabric, white garbage bags, reflector paper, glow-in-the-dark spray paint

Eyes

- Construction paper, felt, poster board, fabrics
- Three-dimensional effect:
  Margarine lids, aerosol cans, Ping-Pong balls
  Plastic moving eyes for smaller figures

COLOR SUGGESTIONS

- Body—white/pastel colors/neon
- Eyes—school colors
- Letters—seasonal/school colors

SLOGANS

- We Have Spirit! Can You Hear It?
- Spirit—You Can Hear It! (Band/music dept.)
- Spirit Moves Our Team

- "School mascot" Spirit Is Everywhere
- "Boo'tiful Halloween Projects
- Spooktacular
- G is for Ghastly Ghouls
- Boo!. . . Don't Be Tricked

ADDITIONAL IDEAS

Ghosts

- Cut letters to place on body of the ghost
- See **Lettering "How-To's"** (pp. 220–29)
- Mix and match faces with bodies
- Reverse ghost patterns for variety
- Ghosts with hands can hold materials: reports, essays, photos, book jackets, music, banner. See **Patterns** (pp. 186–219)

SUGGESTED USES

- School Spirit Week/Pep Club
- Seasonal
- English/Library/Reading (ghost stories/folktales)
- Curriculum
- Clubs/Organizations
- Church Activities

HALLOWEEN
Skeletons

SPECIAL EFFECTS

Skull/Skeleton

- Poster board, foamcore, construction paper, gift box cardboard, plywood, upson board
- Use brass fasteners for movable joints with the following lightweight materials: paper, foamcore, or poster board
- Use bolts to fasten joints with the following heavier materials: plywood and upson board

Directions

This skeleton is made in sections. The sample illustrated shows the basic body parts already connected with paper fasteners. The sections are:

- 1 head
- 1 neck
- 1 upper body
- 1 spine and hip
- 1 upper arm
- 1 hand
- 1 upper leg
- 1 lower leg
- 1 foot

SLOGANS

- Check Out the "Framework"
- Remains to Be Seen
- The Bare Bone Facts
- No Bones About It
- We've Got Spirit
- Success Depends on Backbone
- Let the Spirit Move You
- School Spirit
- A Bone-Crunching Game
- Boning Up (for a Test)

ADDITIONAL IDEAS

Skeletons

- Make life-size (child or adult), use actual clothing: game shirts, cheerleading accessories (megaphones, shirts, pom-poms), sweatshirts, caps, hats, shoes, etc.
- Make freestanding centerpiece with a supporting easel for use on countertops, cabinets, desks, etc.

SUGGESTED USES

- Seasonal
- Curriculum
- School Spirit Week/Sports
- Library/Office/Cafeteria

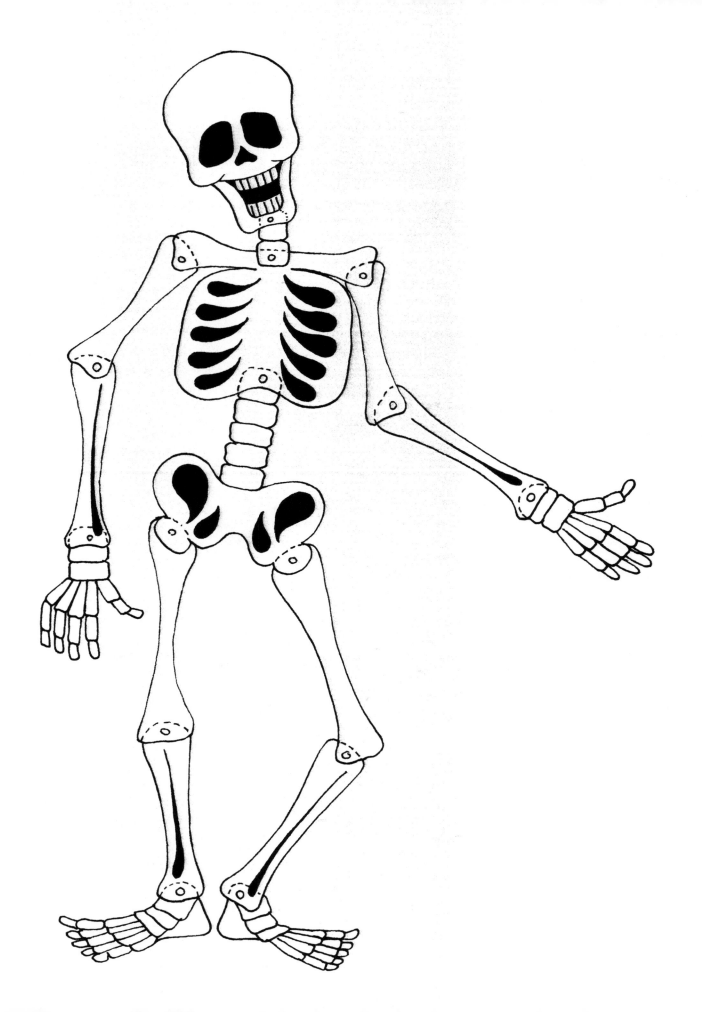

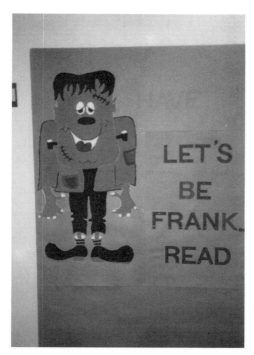

De "monstra"tive! Enough said! (See pp. 28–29.)

Squirrel away today's boards—it could be a long winter (see pp. 34–35).

HALLOWEEN
Frankenstein

SPECIAL EFFECTS

Body

- Construction paper, poster board, foamcore, kraft paper, fabric

Hair

- Felt, fun fur, yarn

Moon

- Construction paper, poster board, foamcore, gold/silver foil, burlap, felt, glossy fabric (silk, lining material, satin)

Blood

- Use rubber cement to glue plastic wrap over red construction paper then cut to size
- Melt wax crayon over cut out drips

COLOR SUGGESTIONS

- Hair—orange/black/green
- Hands/Face—light green
- Jacket—blue/dark green/red
- Pants and shoes—purple/orange/black
- Moon—white/manila/yellow/orange

SLOGANS

- Let's Be Frank. . . . Read (Sing, Dance, Cook, Write, etc.)

- Monster Magic
- Frightfully Good Books to Read
- Just Popping Up . . . To Say "Hi" (To Read, To Sing, To Dance,To Study, etc.)
- Thriller Chiller
- Magic Moments
- Bigger Isn't Always Better. Read Short Stories

ADDITIONAL IDEAS

Body

- Place body to the side, or center on the moon
- Simple black silhouette

Hands

- Hold curriculum materials: book jackets, art work, book reports, etc.

Moon

- With or without drops of blood
- Showcase student works

SUGGESTED USES

- Curriculum
- Seasonal
- Library/Reading (mystery books)
- Clubs/Organizations
- Pep Club/School Spirit Week

HALLOWEEN
Mummy

SPECIAL EFFECTS

Head/Hands

- Construction paper, poster board, foamcore, actual gauze or strips of ripped white fabric glued onto sturdy background, kraft paper

Eyes

- Plastic moving eyes, felt, fabric, transparency film
- Completely cut out the whites of the eyes for hollow 3-D effect

COLOR SUGGESTIONS

- Body Parts/Hair—skin tones, any color

SLOGANS

- Mum's the Word
- Check This Out!
- Get Wrapped Up in . . .
- You're Bound to Learn

- Spooktacular Books (Reports, Arts, etc.)
- Check Out the "Framework"
- Frightfully Good Books to Read

ADDITIONAL IDEAS

Display area

- Use existing bulletin board, door, window, cabinet or wall. Add only face and hands
- Vary hand and face positions
- Use as a peekover

Display use

- Announcements, photographs, book jackets, essays, reports, art work, recipes

SUGGESTED USES

- Seasonal
- Curriculum
- Library/Office/Cafeteria
- Clubs/Organizations
- Church Activities

FALL/THANSKGIVING
Leaves and Tree

SPECIAL EFFECTS

Leaves

- Construction paper, fabric, wrapping paper, colored magazine pages, comics, paper bags, kraft paper, wallpaper, cellophane, colored tissue paper
- Mix handmade with natural materials
- Watercolors, pastels, crayons slivers/shavings ironed and melted waxpaper
- Heavily crayoned typing paper or duplicator paper made to look translucent (for window or mobile display) by rubbing reverse side with cooking oil

Tree

- Construction paper, cardboard, kraft paper, foamcore, gift box cardboard, poster board

COLOR SUGGESTIONS

- Leaves—solid colors or two-toned such as orange/red, yellow/red, yellow/brown, multi-colored
- Tree—brown, black, white, gray, tan

SLOGANS

- Tree-mendous Success in . . . (any subject)
- Falling Favorites (fall leaves and book jackets)

- "Stopping by on a Snowy Day" (bare tree and snowflakes). See **Winter** (pp. 42–55)
- Turn Over a New Leaf (New Year)

ADDITIONAL IDEAS

Tree

- Use basic tree pattern for any season or holiday. Simply change what hangs on the tree. See **Winter** (snowflakes, pp. 44–45), **Valentine's Day** (hearts, pp. 60–63), **Spring** (shamrocks, pp. 70–73)

Single leaves

- As a border, on a tree, falling for windy effect, suspended from ceiling with fishing line

Cluster of leaves

- In corners, baskets, raked pile, or under a tree

SUGGESTED USES

- Seasonal
- Curriculum
- Library/Office/Cafeteria
- Clubs/Organizations
- Church Activities

FALL/THANKSGIVING
Squirrel/Chipmunk

SPECIAL EFFECTS

Body

- Construction paper, poster board, card-board, felt, fun fur, fabric

Leaf

- Kraft paper, construction paper, poster board, felt, fabric, burlap, crayon slivers/shavings ironed and melted between wax paper, magazine pages/covers

COLOR SUGGESTIONS

- Sweater or T-shirt—school colors, yellow-green, yellow, orange, red/orange, red, green
- Body—gray, brown

SLOGANS

- Squirrel Away __?__ Memories
- Fall Into a Good Book (Recipe, Report, Idea, Creative Design)
- Fall Into Reading
- A "Chip" Off the Ol' Book (Classics)

ADDITIONAL IDEAS

Leaf

- Glue burlap or fabric to poster board and curl while glue is wet for three-dimensional effect

Squirrel/Chipmunk

- Place at top of display area over a stack of leaves, student works, book jackets, sheet music, art, school supplies, newspaper articles, magazines, and office memos
- Place along side of a door, between windows, at top corner of a bulletin board

Mobile

- Hang individually or in groups
- Leaves hold slogans, titles, photos, student works
- Use clear fishing line or nylon thread for hanging

SUGGESTED USES

- Seasonal
- Curriculum
- Office/Library/Cafeteria
- Clubs/Organizations
- Church Activities

FALL/THANSKGIVING
Basket

SPECIAL EFFECTS

Basket

- Actual basket, construction paper, poster board, kraft paper, brown paper bag, lightweight cardboard

Apples

- Construction paper, poster board, kraft paper, fabric, felt, contact paper

Basket filler

- Fabric, tissue paper, raffia, bird's nest

Rake

- Actual rake, construction paper, poster board, kraft paper, lightweight cardboard

COLOR SUGGESTIONS

- Basket—natural color, green, brown, tan, gold
- Apples—red, yellow, green
- Flowers—fall: earth tones; spring: pastels

SLOGANS

- It's Harvest Time
- A Basketful of Books (or other materials)
- Sharing Bounty
- A Harvest of Books (or other materials)
- Crisp! Nutritious! Polished and Good! (Each apple displays a book title or a slogan)
- Rake in . . . (A Good Grade)
- A Bushel of Success

ADDITIONAL IDEAS

Basket

Fill with three-dimensional items:
- natural materials such as cattails, dry flowers, leaves, branches, pinecones, thistles, and wheat
- synthetic items such as silk or plastic flowers and leaves
- student works, classroom/library materials, magazine clippings
- seasonal items

Basket—three-dimensional effect

- Cut any type or size basket in half. Fold a 1" by 4" strip of cardboard in half and staple cardboard tabs to cut edges of the basket and then to the bulletin board
- For a textural basket-weave effect—use watered-down paint (peach, light brown, gold, etc.) and brush onto paper in alternating vertical and horizontal strokes

Rake

- Use in combination with basket for any season

Basket Fillers

- Print or paste student names or photos on paper flower centers, leaves, apples, cattails, etc.

SUGGESTED USES

- Curriculum
- Seasonal
- Library/Office/Cafeteria
- Clubs/Organizations
- Church Activities

FALL/THANKSGIVING
Turkey

SPECIAL EFFECTS

Body

- Construction paper, kraft paper, poster board, cardboard, felt, magazine pages/covers

Feathers

- Construction paper, poster board, foamcore, cardboard, fabrics
- Length of feathers approximately the height of the body

COLOR SUGGESTIONS

- Turkey body—brown, black, tan, orange, yellow
- Feathers—same as body, school colors, or applicable to theme

SLOGANS

- Let's Talk Turkey
- Join Us for Thanksgiving
- Gobble Up a Good Book
- Drumstick Days
- "How Can You Soar With Eagles When You Work With Turkeys"?
- We Are Thankful for . . .

ADDITIONAL IDEAS

Feathers

- Fill in with special "thankful" messages, names, classes, events, students' work—drawings, paintings, book reports
- School supplies (designed, cut, or folded to fit), book jackets, art and craft materials (yardsticks, paint brushes, markers, crayons, etc.), sheet music, recipes, kitchen utensils, shop tools, cassette/CD covers
- Clothes—actual clothing such as: mittens, scarves, bandannas, ties, socks, collegiate sweatpants, pennants, theme T-shirts (folded)

Turkey

- Place turkey on scattered leaves, book jackets, or any student works
- Have individuals or a group of students design each feather as a class project

SUGGESTED USES

- Seasonal
- Curriculum
- Library/Office/Cafeteria
- Clubs/Organizations

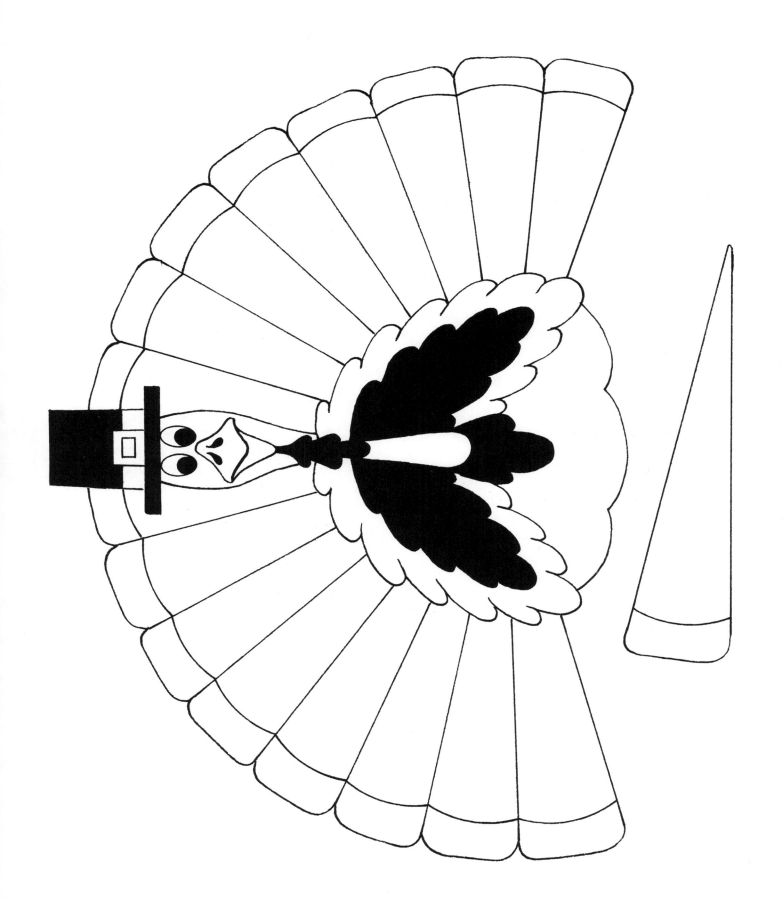

FALL/THANKSGIVING
Pilgrims

SPECIAL EFFECTS

"Kids"

- Construction paper, poster board, foamcore, fabric, felt, gift box cardboard, plywood, upson board
- Use brass fasteners for movable joints with the following lightweight materials: paper, foamcore, or poster board
- Use bolts to fasten joints with the following heavier materials: plywood or upson board

Face/Hands

- Construction paper, poster board, foamcore

Costumes

- Construction paper, poster board, fabric, felt, cardboard

Hat/Belt/Shoes

- Aluminum foil, actual buckles, contact paper, felt, leatherlike fabric

COLOR SUGGESTIONS

Female

- Hat/collar/cuffs/skirt—beige, white, tan, gray, light blue
- Bow/top/shoes—brown, black, navy, or any dark color

Male

- Hat/tunic/socks—rust, green, gold, orange
- Collar/cuffs/pants—beige, white, gray, tan

- Hat band/belt/shoes—brown, black, navy, or any dark color

SLOGANS

- Give Thanks
- Thoughts for Today
- A Pilgrim's Progress
- Sharing Bounty
- Friendship

ADDITIONAL IDEAS

"Kids"

- Hold hands, paper chains of "thankful" messages, banners, flags, pennants, or school items
- Additional hand positions are shown. Patterns can be reversed for left and right hand
- Face variations. See **Patterns** (pp. 186–87)
- Use in pairs to fill a bulletin board, or make smaller for border or favors
- Make freestanding centerpiece with a supporting easel

SUGGESTED USES

- Curriculum
- Office
- Seasonal
- Library

WINTER
Snow "Kids"

SPECIAL EFFECTS

"Kids"

- Construction paper, poster board, foamcore, upson board, 1/4" or luaun plywood, masonite, Styrofoam sheet, fabric, fun fur, wrapping paper, brown kraft paper (gingerbread)
- Use brass fasteners for movable joints with the following lightweight materials: paper, foamcore, or poster board
- Use bolts to fasten joints with the following heavier materials: plywood or upson board

Accessories

- Knit cap, hat, scarf, shovel, ear muffs, gloves, etc.

SLOGANS

- We Hope Your Christmas Hits a Merry Note (Add musical notes or records)
- An Avalanche of Books
- Greetings of the Season
- I'm All Wrapped Up in You! (Hugging)
- I'm Sweet On You (Add candy canes)
- Wintry Wonders

- Snowbound? Read a Book
- A Flurry of Chilly Mysteries
- It's Cool!

ADDITIONAL IDEAS

"Kids"

- Make life-size by using 3/4" to 1" thick Styrofoam, foamcore, or wood
- Use electric carving knife to cut Styrofoam or foamcore
- Change snow "kids" into gingerbread "kids" by using kraft paper or painting other materials brown
- To create snowy effect, try ripping your pattern along the cutting edge
- Some positions will require an "upper" arm

Background

- Add snowflakes, icy border, etc.

SUGGESTED USES

- Seasonal
- Curriculum use—Hold school projects
- Library/Office/Cafeteria
- Clubs/Organizations

WINTER
Snowflakes

NOTE

- Snowflakes are flat, symmetrical, six-pointed crystals. No two are exactly alike
- A circle is 360 degrees. Each section will be divided into 60 degrees to make six sections
- The directions show how to fold paper into six equal sections (60-degree angle). Folding once more will yield a snowflake with twelve points (six major and six minor)

SPECIAL EFFECTS

- Typing paper, tissue, foils, wax paper, duplicator paper, computer paper, lightweight construction paper, wrapping paper
- Spray glue with glitter or artificial snow

DIRECTIONS

- Fold paper in half
- Fold in half again and "pinch" only
- Open and note center pinch
- Fold on a 60-degree angle. Use a 30-60-90 degree plastic triangle as a guide
- Fold in half again for six major and six minor points

- Cut irregular ends to make edges even. The remaining folded form resembles a cone
- Cut any type of design from the center of the cone (shaded area). Cut away sections from folded sides. Important: Leave some folded sections to act as "hinges." See areas marked *

COLOR SUGGESTIONS

- White, pastel blue, pink, lavender, iridescent, metallic

SLOGANS

- Look What's Cool
- A Flurry of Fiction
- Blizzards of Books
- Chill Out!
- Chilly Mysteries

ADDITIONAL IDEAS

- Size can vary depending on use
- Hang individually with fishing line from the ceiling or assemble as a mobile
- Use oversized as display areas

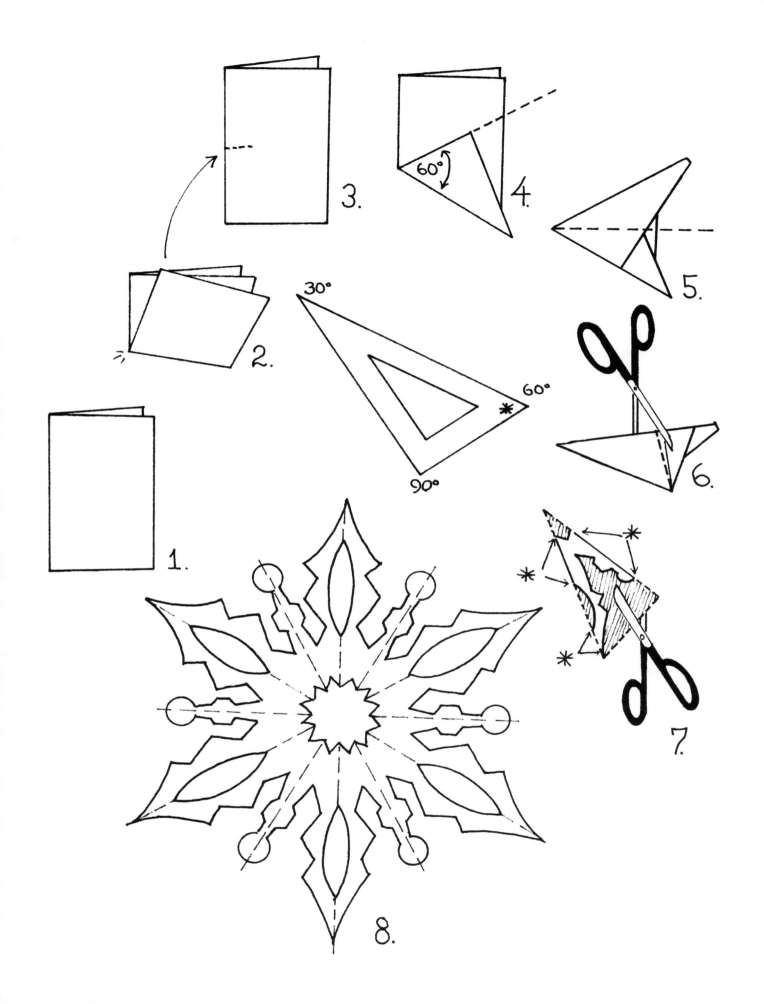

3.

4.

60°

2.

30°

60°

90°

5.

6.

7.

1.

8.

WINTER
Old Man Winter/Icicles

SPECIAL EFFECTS

Man

- Construction paper, foamcore, poster board, kraft paper, foil, fabric, cellophane glued over aluminum foil

Hair

- Yarn, rope, stretched cotton
- Spray glue and glitter

COLOR SUGGESTIONS

- White, blues, violets, grays

SLOGANS

- Look What Just Blew In
- Winter Wonders
- Get the Chill Out
- Frigid Fiction
- A Blizzard of . . . (New Books, Ideas, Recipes, Information)
- Chilly Mysteries
- Arctic Articles
- Shivering Short Stories
- That's Cool!

ADDITIONAL IDEAS

- Border or corner a bulletin board
- Frame a display area
- Lengthen wind to accommodate a slogan or an announcement
- Combine with snowflakes

SUGGESTED USES

- Curriculum/Library
- Office/Cafeteria

ICICLES

Special Effects

- Metallic materials, cellophane rubber cemented over white paper/foil

ADDITIONAL IDEAS

- Border bulletin board, edge desk, doors, counter or display areas
- Hang from window sills or panes
- Make deeper and add "Winter" slogans above icicles. See **Lettering "How-To's"** (pp. 220–29)
- Size and cut icicles to fit any object, letter, tree, ornament, etc.

REPEAT

WINTER
Christmas Tree

SPECIAL EFFECTS

Tree/Letters/Words
- Construction paper, old Christmas cards, wrapping paper, fabric, felt

Treetop Ornament
- Construction paper, old Christmas cards, wrapping paper, aluminum foil wrapped over cardboard, ribbon

COLOR SUGGESTIONS
- Greens, gold, silver
- Seasonal color

ADDITIONAL IDEAS

Tree Outline
- Colored yarn, mini Christmas lights, tinsel, garland
- Use on a door, window, wall

Treetop Ornament
- Substitute with a ribboned bow with multiple streamers, paper bow, angel, commercially made paper bow or treetop ornament

SUGGESTED USES
- Seasonal
- Curriculum
- Library/Office/Cafeteria
- Church Activities
- Clubs/Organizations

WINTER
Holiday Letters

SPECIAL EFFECTS

Letters

- Wrapping paper, colored foils, old Christmas cards, fabrics, felt, wallpaper, magazine pages/covers
- Spray glue with glitter, or use artificial snow
- Glue cotton batting or winter icicles to the top of the letters

Branch

- Artificial garland, painted or cut paper, actual pine or tree branch

COLOR SUGGESTIONS

- Letters—bright colors, metallics, reds, greens
- Branch—greens, blue-green, brown with gold

SLOGANS

Words such as:

- Peace
- Hope
- Joy
- Love
- Peace on Earth
- Noel
- Seasons Greetings
- Happy Hanukkah

ADDITIONAL IDEAS

- Size letters to fill the whole bulletin board
- Use as a border design
- Intermix Christmas words with student names or subjects
- Use foreign language slogans or cultural and ethnic phrases

SUGGESTED USES

- Seasonal
- Curriculum
- Library/Office/Cafeteria
- Clubs/Organizations
- Church Activities

WINTER
Paper Bows

SPECIAL EFFECTS

Bows

- Wrapping paper, construction paper, old Christmas cards, colored magazine pages/covers, wallpaper, foil paper, or any lightweight paper

Thread

- Kite string, yarn, string, embroidery floss

Needle

- Large-eyed darning needle is best

DIRECTIONS

- Cut paper into strips 1"-1 1/2" wide and approximately 8" long. Sizes may vary according to need
- Loop strips in half
- Using needle and thread (yarn and darning needles can be used for young children) sew looped strips together. Use at least 12 loops for a full bow
- Spread loops to make a full bow—gather thread tightly and knot. (Young children may tape ends of thread to last loop.) After knotting or taping, keep remaining thread attached for hanging

COLOR SUGGESTIONS

- Variety of colors or color coordinates
- Harmonize colors to suit seasonal decorations. For example: Fall earth tones or spring pastel colors

ADDITIONAL IDEAS

Bow

- Colored magazine pages/covers—use magazine pages that coordinate in color rather than in subject. Example: Red—ads for spaghetti, Jell-o, Campbell's labels, photos of sunset, fire, etc. Green—ads for vegetables, recipes, gardening articles featuring grass, shrubs, trees, greenery
- Use individually as ornaments or in clusters to make a tree, wreath, bell, or any other holiday shapes
- Mobile
- Have fun decorating. Be creative in finding ways to use these festive bows

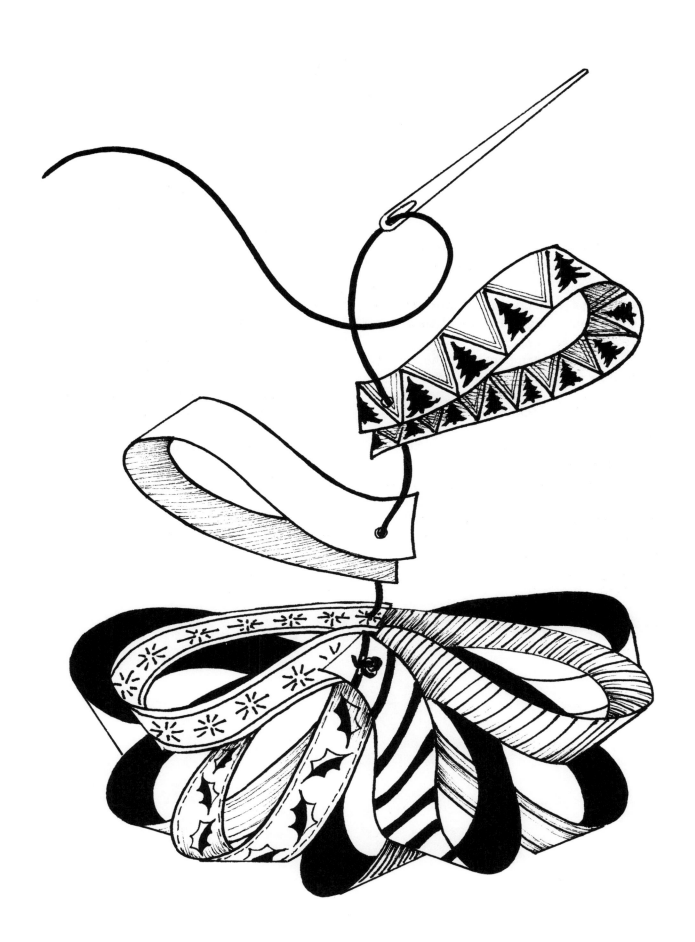

WINTER
Elves

SPECIAL EFFECTS

Body

- Construction paper, poster board, foamcore, fabric, felt, gift box cardboard, plywood, upson board
- Use brass fasteners for movable joints with the following lightweight materials: paper, foamcore, or poster board
- Use bolts to fasten joints with the following heavier materials: plywood or upson board

COLOR SUGGESTIONS

- Body—bright primaries (elf), green (leprechaun)
- Face—peach, white, browns, grays, flesh, tan
- Beard—brown or black (elf), orange or red (leprechaun)
- Gloves/belt/shoes—black

SLOGANS

- Looking for a Mystery
- The Elves and I Are Teaming Up
- We Wish You a Merry Christmas
- 'Tis the Season to Be Jolly

ADDITIONAL IDEAS

Elves

- Students can make their own personal elves
- Reverse hands and legs for variety
- Vary position to stand, walk, run, dance, carry, hold, sit, and climb. Hold tools, craft materials such as paint brushes, scissors, Christmas gifts, snowflakes, student works, etc.
- Convert to leprechauns for St. Patrick's Day

SUGGESTED USES

- Curriculum
- Library/Office/Cafeteria
- Santa's Workshop
- St. Patrick's Day
- Church Activities
- Clubs/Organizations

VALENTINE'S DAY
Heart People

SPECIAL EFFECTS

Hearts

- Construction paper, foamcore, poster board, oaktag, wallpaper, wrapping paper, shelf paper, fabric, felt

Arms/Legs

- Pipe cleaners, accordion-pleated construction paper, felt, yarn, rope, heavy cord, twine

Features

- Felt, plastic moving eyes, magic marker, paint, yarn, fun fur

Accessories

- Bows, ribbons, actual hats/caps, headband, tie, etc.

COLOR SUGGESTIONS

- Hearts—reds, pinks, lavenders, white
- Accessories—school colors, black and white

SLOGANS

- Be a Sweetheart: Pick a Book to Read
- A Heart Full of Love
- The Library (Office, Cafeteria, etc.) Is the Heart of the School
- Be My Valentine

ADDITIONAL IDEAS

People

- Personalize heart people with pennants, pompons, paint brushes, wooden spoons, books, beakers, test tubes, megaphone, sporting/athletic equipment
- Vary hands/feet positions. See **Back-to-School** (pp. 6–9)
- Use small heart "kids" as a border or door decorations
- Individual student caricatures

SUGGESTED USES

- Seasonal
- Curriculum
- Library/Office/Cafeteria
- Church Activities
- Clubs/Organizations

VALENTINE'S DAY
Recipe for Friendship

SPECIAL EFFECTS

Recipe card

- Construction paper, poster board, foamcore, kraft paper, cardboard, fabric, felt, wrapping paper, freezer, or shelf paper

Bowl

- Construction paper, poster board, or for dimensional effects cut thin plastic bowl in half

Hearts

- Cookies, stuffed fabric hearts, modeling clay, dried and varnished bread dough, cardboard, wrapping paper, Valentine cards

COLOR SUGGESTIONS

- Traditional colors or pastels

RECIPE

2 cups of cooperation	1 T friendliness
1 cup of love	1 T understanding
1/2 cup of kisses	1 t compassion
1/2 cup of affection	1/4 t helpfulness
a pinch of calmness	
Serves: All students, faculty, and staff	

Mix in a large, book-filled room—cooperation, love, kisses, and affection. Slowly add friendliness, understanding, compassion, and helpfulness to the mixture. Stir in a pinch of calmness. Mix well with all of your friends. Spread evenly in your life. Bake daily for 365 days at 98.6 degrees for 8 hours. Serve warm and huggable.

Produce wording by handwriting, printing, calligraphy, or computer software program

ADDITIONAL IDEAS

Recipe card
- Use an existing bulletin board
- Use wall space that has been outlined in yarn, colored tape, strips of construction paper or poster board
- Cardboard, kraft paper, fabric—sized to fit the available space

Bowl

- Size of the bowl of hearts can vary depending on the size of the recipe card
- Available space in bowl holds actual treats, cards, student works, supplies, etc.

SUGGESTED USES

- Seasonal
- Curriculum
- Library/Office/Cafeteria
- Church Activities

RECIPE FOR ♥R FRIENDSHIP

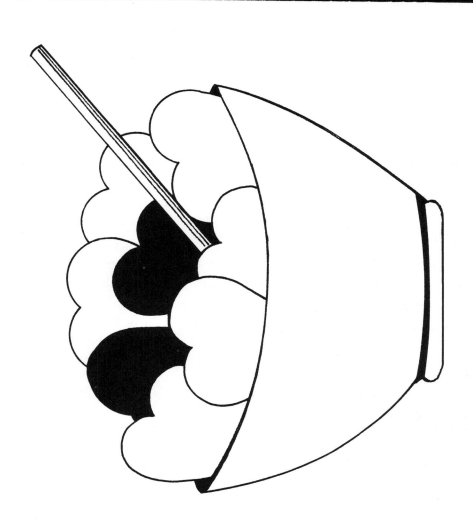

VALENTINE'S DAY
Heart Montage

SPECIAL EFFECTS

Heart

- Construction paper, poster board, foamcore, cardboard, kraft paper

Trim

- Lace, ribbon, doilies, scalloped paper, gathered fabric strips, crepe paper

SLOGANS

- Peace
- Love
- Caring
- Friendship

ADDITIONAL IDEAS

Collage

- Dimensional items—Doilies, lace, ribbons, costume jewelry, silk flowers, or artificial lovebirds

- Use SuperGlue or Goop as an adhesive for 3-D items

Montage

- Articles from magazines and newspapers that represent a theme such as peace, love, friendship, caring, cooperation, giving
- Inside/outside of Valentine cards, wrapping paper, or information on couples in history and literature
- Reproduce sayings, slogans, poetry or songs (photocopy, computer program, calligraphy)
- Use rubber cement as an adhesive

SUGGESTED USES

- Seasonal
- Curriculum
- Library/Office/Cafeteria
- Church Activities
- Clubs/Organizations

VALENTINE'S DAY
Heart Wreath

SPECIAL EFFECTS

Wreath frame

- Construction paper, cardboard, poster board, foamcore, Styrofoam, thin piece of plywood or paneling, wire frame, straw wreath

Hearts

- Construction paper, wrapping paper, colored foil, Valentine card, wallpaper, felt, fabric, colored magazine pages, doilies backed with construction paper

Bow

- Actual bow, ribbon, paper-lace ribbon, crepe paper

ADDITIONAL IDEAS

Wreath

- Window decoration if made two-sided
- Door decoration

Hearts

- Let candy hearts imprinted with messages, such as "Be Mine," inspire additional slogans
- Fill hearts with student works, recipes, reports, etc.
- Recycle this idea by substituting hearts with seasonal patterns such as shamrocks, leaves, flowers, holly, snowflakes, Easter eggs

Frame

- Relocate the bow to lower side or bottom and use wreath as a frame
- Use to showcase student works
- Place slogan inside the frame

SUGGESTED USES

- Curriculum
- Library
- Office/Cafeteria
- Church Organizations
- Seasonal
- Clubs/Organizations

VALENTINE'S DAY
Valen-"Time" Watch

SPECIAL EFFECTS

Watch

- Construction paper, poster board, foamcore, cardboard, Styrofoam, wrapping paper, colored foils

SLOGANS

- "This Is the Time"
- Read Around the Clock
- Anytime Is Reading Time
- Your Time or My Time . . . (to Read, Write, Draw, Sing, etc.)
- Till the End of Time—Read
- Always Time for . . . (Reading, Drawing, Singing, Reading)
- It's Time for Spring
- Time to Read
- Be My Valen-Time
- "Hour" Library Is Great!

ADDITIONAL IDEAS

Watch

- Use for any season by changing heart designs to leaves, shamrocks, snowflakes, or flowers
- Adapt size of watch to fit available display space (examples: on a wall, door, between windows, or in front of teacher's desk, cabinet, etc.)

SUGGESTED USES

- Curriculum
- Library/Office/Cafeteria
- Seasonal
- Church Activities
- Clubs/Organizations

VALENTINE'S DAY
Candy Box

SPECIAL EFFECTS

Candy box

- Construction paper, poster board, oaktag, wrapping paper, fabric, wallpaper
- Actual candy box stapled to bulletin board or as a three-dimensional display on a countertop

Lid

- Decorate with fabric, wrapping paper, Valentine cards, silk flowers, ribbons

COLOR SUGGESTIONS

- Reds, pinks, white, lavenders, soft pastels

SLOGANS

- Be a Sweetheart: Pick a Book to Read
- I'm in Love with . . . (Reading, Books, Curriculum subjects)
- When It Comes to Your Heart—Read
- A Heart Full of Love
- The Library Is the Heart of the School
- Life (Reading) Is Like a Box of Chocolates (Forrest Gump)

ADDITIONAL IDEAS

Filler

- Fill box with students' works, projects, essays, book jackets, classroom materials
- Silk flowers, silk lining, colored tissue paper
- Elementary—photographs of students, poetry, slogans of peace
- Secondary—dance announcements, souvenirs of prom dance, friendship notes

SUGGESTED USES

- Seasonal
- Curriculum
- Library/Office/Cafeteria
- Church Activities
- Clubs/Organizations

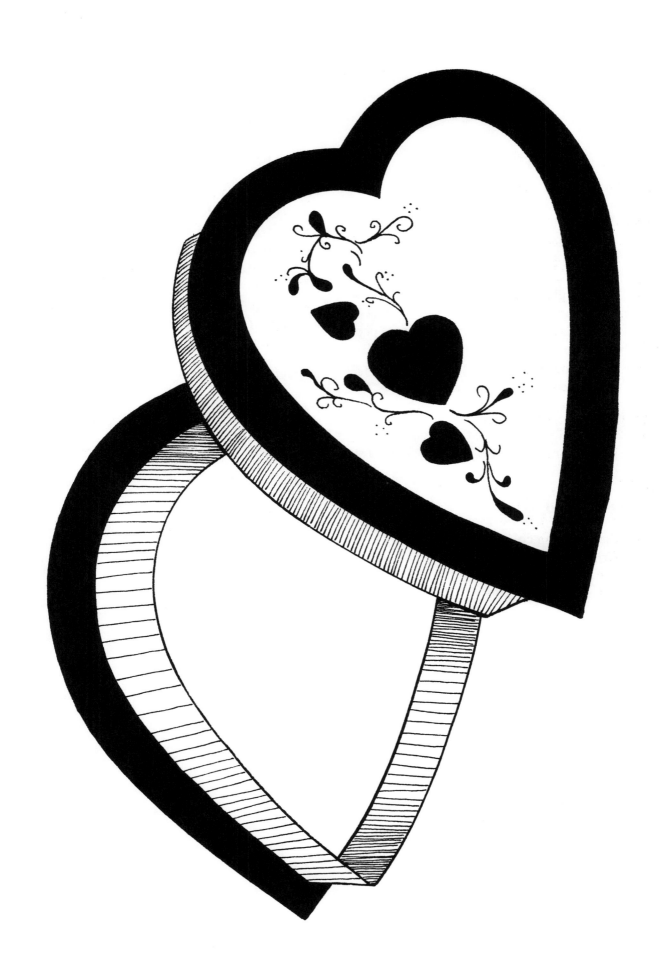

SPRING
Kites

SPECIAL EFFECTS

Kites

- Actual working kites with thin wood strips, tissue paper, and cotton string. Paint with inks or watercolors
- Commercially made kites or windsocks
- Stained-glass effect—use black construction paper for butterfly body outline. Cut out white areas (*) and glue colored tissue paper to the outline
- Wrapping paper, wallpaper, lightweight fabrics, construction paper

Bows

- Twist strips of colored tissue around string
- Ribbon bows, "twisted paper," or construction paper

COLOR SUGGESTIONS

- Pastel spring colors
- Bright neon colors

SLOGANS

- Spring Is Flying High
- Hitch Your Reading to a Kite
- Stories Above and Beyond
- Stay on Top of the Action
- Get Carried Away—Read (Write, Draw, etc.)
- Up in the Air? Books Can Help Solve Problems (kite tails are book titles)
- Into the Wild Blue Yonder

ADDITIONAL IDEAS

- Mobiles
- Hung individually from the ceiling with fishing line

SUGGESTED USES

- Seasonal
- Curriculum, especially Science
- Library/Office/Cafeteria
- Clubs/Organizations
- Church Activities

SPRING
Cauldron/Rainbow/Shamrock Tree

SPECIAL EFFECTS

Rainbow

- Lines: plastic or electrical tape, rug yarn
- Spaces: cellophane or colored tissue paper, construction paper, colored pastels blended on white kraft paper

Cauldron

- Black poster board for outside with light colored construction paper or metallic foil on the inside

SLOGANS

- In Every Book There's a Pot of Gold
- You'll Find Gold at the End of the Rainbow
- Good Luck, Charm!
- Books Add Color to Your Life
- A Spectrum of Stories (Reports, Essays, etc.)

ADDITIONAL IDEAS

Rainbow

- Display slogans, student works
- Use as a musical staff with notes or words

Cauldron

- Holds gold coins, book jackets, teaching materials, photographs, etc.

Tree

- See **Fall/Thanksgiving** (pp. 32–33) for special effects, color suggestions, slogans, and additional ideas

SUGGESTED USES

- Curriculum
- Library/Office/Cafeteria
- Clubs/Organizations
- Seasonal
- Curriculum, Especially Science
- Library/Office/Cafeteria
- Clubs/Organizations
- Church Activities

SPRING
Leprechaun

SPECIAL EFFECTS

Body

- Construction paper, poster board, foamcore, fabric, felt, gift box cardboard, plywood, upson board
- Use brass fasteners for movable joints with the following lightweight materials: paper, foamcore, or poster board
- Use bolts to fasten joints with the following heavier materials: plywood or upson board

Clothing material

- Construction paper, fabric, wallpaper, felt, contact paper, school blotters (green)

Hair

- Construction paper, burlap, felt, fun fur, yarn, sandpaper

Mushrooms

- Cardboard, kraft paper, gift box cardboard, wallpaper, fabric

COLOR SUGGESTIONS

- Leprechaun—greens, school colors
- Beard—red, orange, brown, white
- Mushrooms—tan, brown, white

SLOGANS

- Sing (Paint, Dance, Read, etc.) With the Leprechaun(s)

- Keep in Step With March
- Search for the Shamrocks
- It's a Topsy-Turvy World
- Anyway You Look at It (subject) Is Fun
- I'm Head-Over-Heels in Love With You
- I've Flipped Over You!
- Dance With the Leprechauns
- "When Irish Hearts Are Happy"
- Search for the Lucky Shamrocks. Read a Book
- Read With the Leprechauns

ADDITIONAL IDEAS

Mushrooms

- Use as display areas for letters, slogans, student works
- See **Back-to-School** (pp. 2–15) and **Lettering "How-To's"** (pp. 220–29)

Leprechauns

- Hold books, pencils, pens, papers, pennants, baton, hammer, etc.
- Vary positions to suggest: standing, playing, working, dancing, tumbling, etc.

SUGGESTED USES

- Seasonal
- Curriculum
- Library/Office/Cafeteria

SPRING
Duck

SPECIAL EFFECTS

Duck

- Construction paper, poster board, foamcore, wrapping paper, fabric, fun fur, felt

Boots/Umbrella/Hat

- Actual child-sized accessories
- Colored vinyl, cellophane rubber cemented over construction paper

Puddle/Raindrops

- Aluminum foil, clear contact paper, transparency film, plastic wrap rubber cemented to blue construction paper, laminated paper for the "wet" look

COLOR SUGGESTIONS

- Duck—yellow/white body, orange/yellow beak
- Accessories—bright neon colors such as kelly green, yellow, red, royal blue/red for hat/umbrella/boots

SLOGANS

- Duck Out of the Rain—Read a Book (or Work on Projects, Throw a Pot, Use the Computer)
- Don't Dampen Your Skills
- Drop in for a Shower of Reading (Writing, Math Skills, Computer Programming)
- Showers of New Books (Skills, Projects, Activities, Games)
- It's Just Ducky
- Track in . . .
- Thaw . . .
- Melt . . .

ADDITIONAL IDEAS

Footprints

- Make same size as duck boots

Letters

- See **Lettering "How-To's"** (pp. 220–29)

Duck Wing

- Cut along dotted line to hold a book jacket, photos, student projects, an announcement, or lightweight classroom item

SUGGESTED USES

- Seasonal
- Curriculum, Especially Science
- Library/Office/Cafeteria
- Clubs/Organizations
- Church Activities

SPRING
Rain/Mystery Man

SPECIAL EFFECTS

Man

- Construction paper, poster board, kraft paper, foamcore, luaun plywood

Accessories

- Actual rain cap or trench coat, construction paper, poster board, kraft paper, fabric, garbage bag

Raindrops/puddles

- Aluminum foil, clear contact paper, transparency film, laminated construction paper for the "wet" look or plastic wrap rubber cemented to blue construction paper

Mustache

- Fun fur, yarn, costume moustache, black paper, pipe cleaners, marker

COLOR SUGGESTIONS

- Gray/brown/tan trench coat
- Black for mystery man

SLOGANS

- Dial M for Mystery
- Want to Try Something Mysterious?
- Start the Search

- Looking for a Good Mystery?
- Mysterious! Criminally Entertaining
- Booked for Murder
- Get the Chills—Read a Mystery
- Don't Dampen Your Skills
- Drop in on (for) a Shower of Reading (Writing, Math Skills)
- Showers of New Books (Skills, Projects, Activities, Games)
- Don't Let Mother Nature Get You Down
- Discover . . . (Books, etc.)
- The Mystery Is in Not Knowing

ADDITIONAL IDEAS

Body

- Size to fit a door, between windows or any available bulletin board space

Face

- See **Patterns** (pp. 186–87)

SUGGESTED USES

- Mystery man/Rain man with happy or gloomy effect
- Curriculum
- Library/Office/Cafeteria
- Clubs/Organizations
- Church Activities

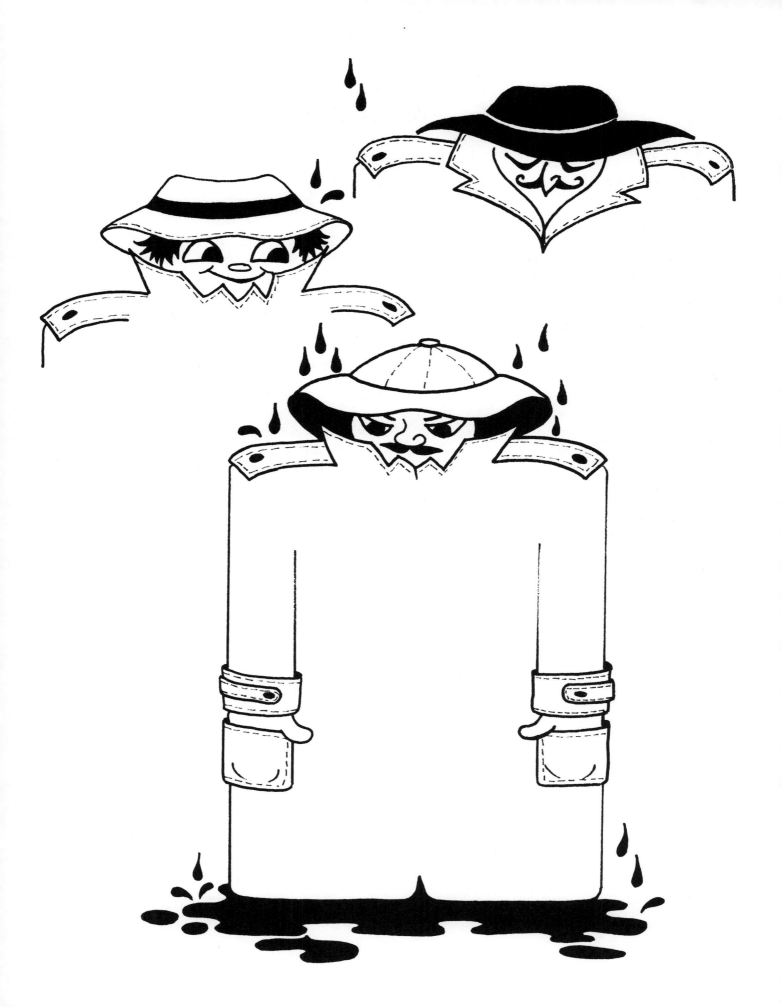

SPRING
Daffodil

SPECIAL EFFECTS

Flower

- Construction paper, poster board, fabric, foamcore, wrapping paper, artcraft paper, wallpaper, tissue paper

Grassy area

- Construction paper, crepe paper, felt, green desk blotters

COLOR SUGGESTIONS

- Flowers—orange, yellow, white, gold, pink

ADDITIONAL IDEAS

Grassy area

- Extend vertically or horizontally to fit available display space

Daffodils

- Use any vertical letter stroke as a daffodil stem
- Side-view daffodil trumpet announces spring projects, research papers, exhibits, books to read, concerts
- Front-view daffodil trumpet center displays photos, papers, slogans, student works, etc.

Words

- See **Lettering "How-To's"** (pp. 220–29)

SUGGESTED USES

- Curriculum, Especially Science
- Seasonal
- Library/Office/Cafeteria
- Church Activities
- Clubs/Organizations

WORK SHOP

SPRING HAS SPRUNG - SPRING HAS SPRUNG

SPRING
Reading Rabbits

SPECIAL EFFECTS

Rabbit

- Construction paper, poster board, fun fur, fabric, freezer paper, cotton batting, felt

Whiskers

- Pipe cleaners, broom bristles, telephone wire, cord, string, yarn

Books

- Construction paper, poster board, foamcore, wrapping paper, actual book jackets or books

COLOR SUGGESTIONS

- Rabbit—pink, white, tan, brown

SLOGANS

- Hop to and Stop at . . . (Your Library)
- Hop to the Library
- Books That Will Hop Off the Shelves

- "Hare" Comes Easter
- Don't Be a Dumb Bunny—Read (Write, Draw, Think, etc.)

ADDITIONAL IDEAS

Rabbits

- Repeat as a border design
- Use over a door, window ledge, or counter-top
- Make as a freestanding centerpiece with a supporting easel
- Use as peekovers
- Remove, add, or interchange hands, feet, faces for variety

SUGGESTED USES

- Seasonal, especially for Easter
- Curriculum, especially for Reading
- Library/Cafeteria/Office
- Clubs/Organizations
- Church Activities

SPRING
Top Hat/Rabbit

SPECIAL EFFECTS

Hat

- Fabric such as silk, satin, felt, leatherlike materials

Objects

- Use three-dimensional, lightweight objects. Media: CDs, filmstrips, small movie reels; Art: brushes, crayons, scissors, erasers, rulers; Math: protractors, triangles, pencils, rulers; Playing cards, Catalog cards

Rabbit

- Construction paper, foamcore, felt, fun fur, freezer paper, cotton batting

COLOR SUGGESTIONS

- Hat—school colors, black, white
- Rabbit—pink, white, tan, brown

SLOGANS

- Escape With a Good Book
- For That Magic Touch
- Another Opening, Another Show
- Looking for a Good Mystery?
- Media Magic
- Play It Straight! (Drug slogan)
- It's Magic

ADDITIONAL IDEAS

Open house

- Add block letters on elongated hat to spell out welcome. See **Lettering "How-To's"** (pp. 220–29). Display school projects and student works falling out of hat

Prom time

- Photographs of couples, mementos, programs, flavors, theme/slogan of the prom, etc., falling out of the hat

Cafeteria/Nutrition class

- Eat-right recipes and menus, weight watching tips falling out of the hat

SUGGESTED USES

- Open House/Welcome
- Prom
- Seasonal
- Curriculum, especially Family and Consumer Services
- Library, especially mystery theme
- Clubs/Organizations
- Church Activities

SPRING
Invisible Rabbit

SPECIAL EFFECTS

Rabbit

- Construction paper, poster board, felt, fun fur, foamcore, fabric, freezer paper, cotton batting

Accessories

- Actual bow tie

Whiskers

- Pipe cleaners, broom bristles, telephone wire, cord, string, yarn

COLOR SUGGESTIONS

- Rabbit—pink, white, tan, brown

SLOGANS

- Hop to and Stop at . . . Your library
- Hop to the Library
- Books That Will Hop Off the Shelves
- Hare Comes Easter
- Don't Be a Dumb Bunny . . . (Read, Write, Draw, Think, etc.)

ADDITIONAL IDEAS

Rabbit

- Use for magic themes. See **Top Hat/Rabbit** (pp. 82–83)

Display area

- Use existing bulletin board, door, window, cabinet, or wall and add head, hands, and feet
- Vary hand and face positions
- Use as a peekover

Display Use

- Announcements, photographs, book jackets, essays, reports, art work, recipes

SUGGESTED USES

- Seasonal
- Curriculum
- Library/Office/Cafeteria
- Clubs/Organizations
- Church Activities

SPRING
Fishing/Rod and Reel

SPECIAL EFFECTS

Rod and reel

- An actual rod and reel, construction paper, poster board, dowel rod, heavy cardboard, foamcore (reel)

Fish

- Iridescent wrapping paper, colored foil paper, poster board, kraft paper, water-colored paper

Water drops

- Blue cellophane or foil, blue plastic wrap over aluminum foil, transparency film
- Laminated paper for the "wet" look

Bubbles

- Hole punch-outs

COLOR SUGGESTIONS

- Realistic fish—brown, iridescent, green. Use colored pastels and blend softly. Fix with hair spray
- Graphic fish—primary and secondary colors, metallic, neon

SLOGANS

- Fish for Fiction
- Some Books Are "Fishy"
- Fishing for a Good Book/Better Grades
- Gone Fishing for a Book
- Catch This!
- Get Your Limit!
- Fishing Around for a Good Pastime/Hobby/Career

ADDITIONAL IDEAS

Rod and reel

- Frame a bulletin board, door, or window
- Use on blank wall to create a display area

Background

- "Sandwich" rubber cement between two layers of plastic wrap

Fish

- Color with bright watercolors, poster paints, or pastels
- Outline "wet-into-wet" designs with black marker
- Borders, display areas, name tags, mobiles

SUGGESTED USES

- Curriculum, especially Science
- Seasonal
- Library/Office/Cafeteria
- Clubs/Organizations
- Church Activities

SPRING
Fishing/Bobbin and Hook

SPECIAL EFFECTS

Water (wet effect)

- Laminated paper, cellophane, aluminum foil, or sandwich a generous amount of rubber cement between colored foil and clear plastic wrap, transparency film

Bottom of tank

- Actual sand and small pebbles, kraft paper, felt, fabrics
- Cut sandpaper

Bobbin

- Whole or half of an actual bobbin
- Styrofoam ball cut in half

Line/Hook

- Actual fishing line and hook, string, yarn, thread, paper clip, wire

Underwater life

- Construction paper, felt, sandpaper, ribbon, tissue paper, rickrack, trims, crepe paper, foil, bubble wrap

SLOGANS

- Get Hooked With a Good Book
- Caught Any Good Books Lately?
- Book Bait to Hook Readers
- People Get Hooked on Us
- Take a Nibble! Read!
- Get Hooked!
- Hook a Good Book
- Catch This . . . (Job, Career, etc.)
- Catch Your Limit

ADDITIONAL IDEAS

Fish

- Add fish to display student projects, book jackets, etc. See **Fishing/Rod and Reel** (pp. 86–87)

Aquarium

- Convert bulletin board, cabinet or counter front, door, or any wall space into a display area
- Use as a window display, especially effective if transparent (cellophane, plastic wrap) or translucent (tissue paper, oil-rubbed crayoned papers) materials are used

SUGGESTED USES

- Curriculum, especially Science/Nature
- Seasonal
- Library/Office/Cafeteria
- Clubs/Organizations
- Church Activities

GRADUATION
Graphic

SPECIAL EFFECTS

Body

- Construction paper, poster board, foamcore, cardboard, kraft paper, fabric, felt, gift box cardboard, plywood, upson board

Cap/Gown

- Fabric, felt, construction paper, poster board, contact paper, shelf paper, actual cap/gown

Accessories

- Construction paper, fabric, parchment paper, felt, actual bow tie

Tassel

- Yarn, embroidery floss, chandelier pull chain, drapery tieback, actual school tassel

COLOR SUGGESTIONS

- School colors
- Black and white (formal look)

SLOGANS

- Full Steam Ahead!
- We Are Moving On! Good Luck!
- We Can't Have Success Without U
- Moving On!
- "You've Come a Long Way, Baby"
- Challenge and Change
- School's Over!

ADDITIONAL IDEAS

Body

- Use for prom or graduation
- Show a transition from student to prom participant to graduate
- Use as a display area for pictures, photos, mementos, academic work, honor roll
- Size to fit a door, between windows, or any vertical/narrow display space

SUGGESTED USES

- Seasonal
- Curriculum
- Library/Office/Cafeteria
- Clubs/Organizations
- Church Activities
- Guidance Office

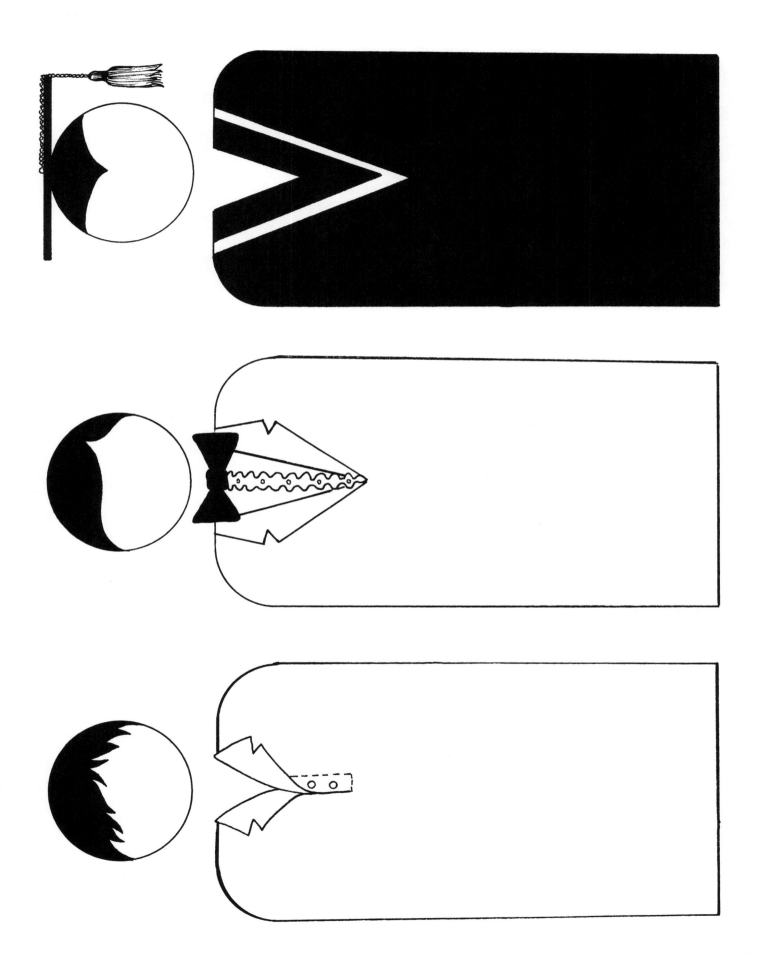

GRADUATION
Realistic

SPECIAL EFFECTS

"Grad Kid"

- Construction paper, poster board, foamcore, cardboard, kraft paper, fabric, felt, gift box cardboard, plywood, upson board
- Use brass fasteners for movable joints with the following lightweight materials: paper, foamcore, or poster board
- Use bolts to fasten joints with the following heavier materials: plywood or upson board

Accessories

- Construction paper, fabric, parchment paper, felt, actual pennant or school supplies

Cap/Gown

- Fabric, felt, construction paper, poster board, contact paper, shelf paper, actual cap/gown

Tassel

- Yarn, embroidery floss, chandelier pull chain, drapery tieback, actual school tassel

Collar

- Colored foil, shiny fabric

COLOR

- Traditional school colors
- Black and white for formal use

SLOGANS

- Stop, Look, School Ahead
- Are You Ready for College? (Job, Military Service)
- When You Grow Up!—?
- What's Next?
- Moving On!

ADDITIONAL IDEAS

"Grad Kid"

- Make as a freestanding centerpiece with a supporting easel
- Make smaller and use as a border, invitation, or favor (individually made by students)
- Carry school items, hold paper chains of graduation messages, a banner, flag, or pennant
- Can be male or female. See **Patterns** (pp. 188–95) and **Back-to-School** (pp. 6–9)
- Personalize with hairstyle, hair color, eye color
- Stand on books, signposts, college pennants, or banners that announce career or college choices

SUGGESTED USES

- Seasonal
- Library/Office/Cafeteria
- Clubs/Organizations
- Church Activities

SUMMER
Beach Guy

SPECIAL EFFECTS

Beach towel

- Kraft paper, construction paper, shelf paper, contact paper, freezer paper, wallpaper, wrapping paper, actual beach towel

Bathing suit

- Construction paper, wrapping paper, shelf paper, wallpaper, magazine photo montage, actual trunks

Sunglasses

- Cardboard, construction paper, aluminum foil, cellophane, black garbage bag plastic, actual sunglasses

Beach guy

- Construction paper, cardboard, kraft paper, freezer paper

Beach

- Sandpaper, brown kraft paper, sprinkled with sand and spray glued

COLOR SUGGESTIONS

- Bright colors that are in style
- School colors

SLOGANS

- Stretch Yourself This Summer (a career bulletin board)
- Get Into the Swim With Books
- Books for Summer Days
- Stretch Out—Read (Create, Sew, Draw, Write)
- Stretch Into Summer Reading
- Hot Summer Reading
- Extend Your Knowledge—Read
- Find the Far-Reaching Effects of Reading
- Spread the News!

ADDITIONAL IDEAS

Layout

- Vertical position—place beach guy next to a doorway, on a door, between windows, or any vertical/narrow display space
- Horizontal position—place beach guy over a bulletin board, under a counter, or on a bulkhead

Bathing suit

- Montage of magazine or theme photos: such as summer sports, seascapes, fishing, camping, summer fashions, vacation spots, summer studies, hobbies

SUGGESTED USES

- Seasonal
- Curriculum
- Library/Office/Cafeteria
- Clubs/Organizations
- Church Activities

SUMMER
Clothesline

SPECIAL EFFECTS

Clothesline

- Rope, rug yarn, twine, braided telephone or picture wire, braided yarn, actual clothesline

Clothes

- Construction paper, poster board, kraft paper, fabric, felt, wrapping paper, actual clothes (especially denim)

Accessories

- Clothespins, paperbacks, book jackets, school supplies, craft and hobby materials

COLOR SUGGESTIONS

- Clothes—popular styles, seasonal colors, denim
- Background—light blue, yellow, pastel colors

SLOGANS

- Hang Onto Reading Skills This Summer
- Hang in There. Summer Is Coming!
- Denim Blues? . . . Read (Write, Sew, Saw)
- Hip-Pocket Reading
- Don't Be Hung Up; Hang Onto a Book
- Get Hip—Read!

ADDITIONAL IDEAS

Clothes

- Vary with season and style
- Purchase inexpensively at flea markets or thrift shops

Background (not illustrated)

- Light solid color
- Horizon line with sky and land colors
- Add sun and sun rays

Display area

- Create an area with stretched clothesline

SUGGESTED USES

- Seasonal
- Curriculum
- Library/Office/Cafeteria
- Clubs/Organizations
- Church Activities

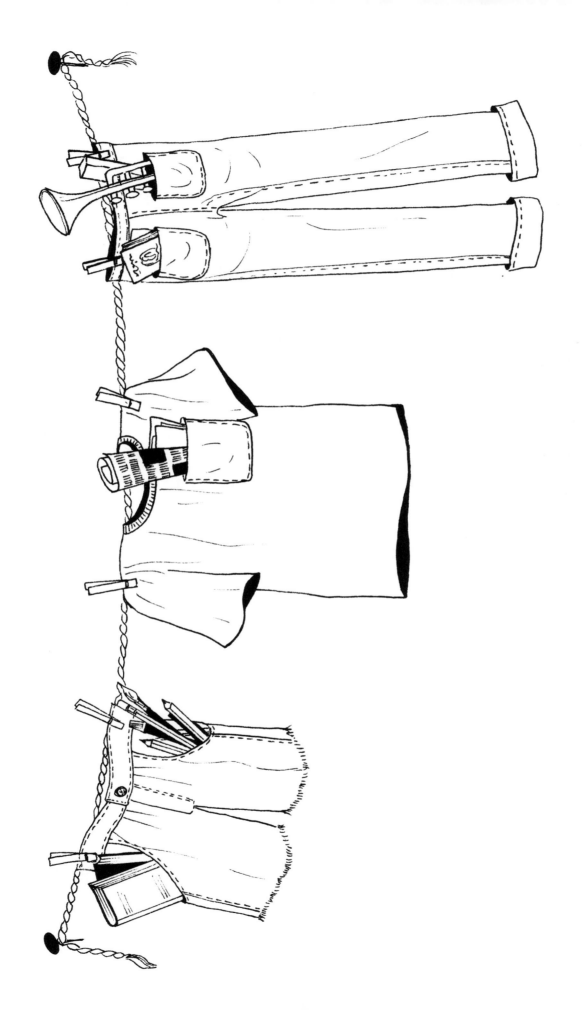

READING
Reading Teddy Bear

SPECIAL EFFECTS

Teddy bear

- Construction paper, poster board, gift box cardboard, foamcore, kraft paper, felt, fabrics, luaun plywood, 1/4" masonite, fun fur, leatherlike materials

Paws

- Construction paper, poster board, fabrics such as: calico, dotted swiss, gingham

Accessories

- Ribbon for bows in hair or around neck
- Necktie, bow tie, barrettes, baby bib, etc.

COLOR SUGGESTIONS

- Brown, black, tan, white, black and white
- Bright, bold colors

SLOGANS

- Sink your Claws Into a Book
- Footprints to a Great Year
- Books Cannot Bear to Go Unread
- The "Bear" Essentials—Books and Reading
- A Li-bear-y Adventure
- Who Can Bear Not to Read?
- Make Tracks

ADDITIONAL IDEAS

Bear

- Make freestanding by using heavier materials (foamcore) and a supporting easel

Smaller-sized bear

- Borders, stacked on top of each other, floating with a balloon, and reading/studying

SUGGESTED USES

- Curriculum
- Library/Office/Cafeteria
- Clubs/Organizations
- Church Activities

READING
Hinged Teddy Bear

SPECIAL EFFECTS

Teddy bear

- Construction paper, poster board, gift box cardboard, foamcore, kraft paper, felt, fabric, luaun plywood, 1/4" masonite, fun fur, leatherlike materials
- Use brass fasteners for movable joints with the following lightweight materials: paper, foamcore, or poster board
- Use bolts to fasten joints with the following heavier materials: plywood, or upson board

Paws

- Construction paper, poster board, fabrics such as: calico, dotted swiss, gingham

Accessories

- Fabric, felt, actual clothing, hats

COLOR SUGGESTIONS

- Brown, black, tan, white, black and white
- Bright, bold colors

SLOGANS

- Bear With Us—We're New Here
- In-fur-mation
- This Is Teddy Bear Territory/Country
- _____Are Beary Special
- Being With You Makes Me Warm and Fuzzy
- Bear Necessities
- Bear-O-Meter

ADDITIONAL IDEAS

Bear

- Make groupings of bears and vary positions to suggest: running, playing, dancing, jumping, floating, diving, etc.
- Mix and match arms, legs, and faces

SUGGESTED USES

- Curriculum
- Library/Office/Cafeteria
- Clubs/Organizations
- Church Activities

You can now "commence" to successful bulletin boards! (See pp. 90–91)

One of our cool ideas! (See pp. 118–19)

READING
Announcements

SPECIAL EFFECTS

Horns

- Construction paper, metallic paper, foil, gift box cardboard, poster board, oaktag

Banner

- Fabric, felt, wrapping paper, wall paper, freezer paper, kraft paper, contact paper, shelf paper

Fanfare

- Cording, tape, rope, yarn, twine

COLOR SUGGESTIONS

- Metallics
- School colors
- Seasonal colors

SLOGANS

- Jazz Up Your Study Skills (or any subject)
- In Tune With Art (any subject)

- Announcing New Books (any subject)
- New Arrivals
- Celebrate the Spirit
- Let's Celebrate

ADDITIONAL IDEAS

Inside solid horn/banner

- Use as a display area

Letter horn

- Change lettering to school initials, date, time, exclamatory words such as "Wow," "Great," etc.

SUGGESTED USES

- Curriculum
- Library/Office/Cafeteria
- Clubs/Organizations
- Church Activities
- Back-to-School

READING
New Arrivals

SPECIAL EFFECTS

Stork

- Construction paper, poster board, freezer paper, shelf paper, fun fur, felt, fabric, oaktag

Chick

- Construction paper, poster board, freezer paper, shelf paper, fun fur, felt, fabric, oaktag

Shell

- Foamcore, poster board

Diaper

- Construction paper, poster board, freezer paper, shelf paper, fun fur, felt, fabric, actual diaper

COLOR SUGGESTIONS

- Stork—white
- Chick—white, yellow, cream
- Diaper—white, pastels
- Baby—skin tones

SLOGANS

Storks/Diaper

- Look What's New
- New Additions
- Additional Ideas
- It's New! It's Novel!

- What's New
- Books That Fill the Bill

Chick

- Don't Be an Egghead
- Scramble for Good Grades
- Look What's New

ADDITIONAL IDEAS

Stork

- Carry books, school supplies, educational materials, etc.
- Actual eyeglasses

Chick

- Substitute chick with books, school supplies, educational materials, slogans, song titles, etc., and fill in with tissue paper, wrapping paper, or confetti
- Use for Easter

Diaper

- Carry books, school supplies, educational materials, etc.

SUGGESTED USES

- Curriculum
- Library/Office/Cafeteria
- Clubs/Organizations
- Seasonal, Especially Easter or Spring

READING
Reading Worms

SPECIAL EFFECTS

Worms

- Construction paper, magazine pages or covers, kraft paper, felt, fun fur, fabric, foamcore, wrapping paper, wallpaper, colored burlap

Antennae

- Wire, pipe cleaners, heavy yarn, rope, pompoms, Styrofoam balls, Ping-Pong balls

Eyes/Glasses

- Construction paper, poster board, cellophane, waxpaper, transparency film, foil, large moving eyes, fabric, felt, actual glasses

Book

- Construction paper, poster board, kraft paper, oaktag, foamcore, fabric, gift box cardboard, felt, wrapping paper, shelf paper, wallpaper, actual book jacket

COLOR SUGGESTIONS

- Worms—greens, browns, orange, yellows, any bright color
- Glasses—black, brown, metallic
- Book—neutrals, white, grays, tan, black, primary, seasonal

SLOGANS

- Worm Your Way Into a Good Book
- Be a Book Worm
- Read All About It!
- Read On, Babbling Bookworm
- Worm Your Way Into One of These
- Have You Read This? (These?)
- What Should I Read?

ADDITIONAL IDEAS

Worms

- Add segments until the worm reaches a predetermined destination
- Tape string to back of worm sections and stretch across walls or ceilings
- Use segments as display areas for book titles, book reports, student works, teaching materials, etc.

Spotted worm

- Use as shown or lengthen by adding extra humps
- Use above door, window, lockers, storage cabinets
- Use on a desk, shelf, or countertop
- Make freestanding by using foamcore, Styrofoam, upson board, masonite, luaun plywood, or any heavy material. Add easel to back
- Three-dimensional effect—fold accordion style

SUGGESTED USES

- Curriculum
- Clubs/Organizations
- Library/Office
- Church Activities

READING
Reading "Kids"

SPECIAL EFFECTS

"Kids"

- Construction paper, poster board, kraft paper, oaktag, foamcore, fabric, gift box cardboard

Hair

- Yarn, fun fur, rope, felt, fabric, rubber matting

Books

- Construction paper, poster board, kraft paper, oaktag, foamcore, fabric, gift box cardboard, felt, wrapping paper, shelf paper, wallpaper, actual book jackets

COLOR SUGGESTIONS

- Faces—skin tones
- Hair—natural, brights
- Books—neutrals, white, grays, tan, black, primary, seasonal

SLOGANS

- Get Wrapped Up in Reading
- Kids Who Read—Succeed

- What Are You Reading?
- Hug Me—Read Me
- Learn to Discern
- Bury Your Head in a Book
- Are You All Booked Up?

ADDITIONAL IDEAS

"Kids"

- Use any of our "kids" for a variety of faces, hairstyles, and positions (see **Patterns,** pp. 196–203)

Books

- Use as display areas

Hats

- Change the effect by adding a hat (see **Patterns,** pp. 196–203) for careers, sports and multicultural examples.

SUGGESTED USES

- Curriculum
- Library/Office/Cafeteria
- Clubs/Organizations
- Church Activities
- Sports/Pep Club

READING
Exercise "Kid" 1

SPECIAL EFFECTS

"Kid"

- Construction paper, poster board, kraft paper, foamcore, fabric, felt, upson board, plywood, actual clothing
- Use brass fasteners for movable joints with the following lightweight materials: paper, foamcore, or poster board
- Use bolts to fasten joints with the following heavier materials: plywood and upson board

Books

- Construction paper, poster board, kraft paper, oaktag, actual book jackets, wrapping paper, gift box cardboard, actual gift boxes, fabric, felt

COLOR SUGGESTIONS

- "Kid"—skin tones
- Clothing—seasonal, school, or team colors

SLOGANS

- Reading "Jogs" Your Mind
- Shape Up Your Reading (Behavior, Art Skills, Body, Mind)
- "Let's Get Physical!"
- Feel Sharp, Be Sharp—Read!
- Reading IS NOT Hazardous to Your Health
- Read for the Fun of It

ADDITIONAL IDEAS

Kid

- Use alone as shown, or lengthen pole and add more exercise "kids"
- Hinged kids provide creative positioning
- Use face and hands only as a peekover

Books

- Three-dimensional—stack gift boxes covered with wrapping paper, book jackets, or book covers
- Frame a display area by using book columns
- Substitute books with school materials and supplies (computer disks, cassettes, CDs, tools, etc.), sports equipment, or club items

SUGGESTED USES

- Curriculum, especially Physical Education
- Library/Office/Cafeteria
- Clubs/Organizations
- Guidance/Counselor

READING
Exercise "Kid" 2

SPECIAL EFFECTS

"Kid"

- Construction paper, poster board, kraft paper, foamcore, fabric, felt, upson board, plywood, actual clothing
- Use brass fasteners for movable joints with the following lightweight materials: paper, foamcore, or poster board
- Use bolts to fasten joints with the following heavier materials: plywood and upson board

COLOR SUGGESTIONS

- "Kid"—skin tones
- Clothing—seasonal, school, or team colors

SLOGANS

- Reading "Jogs" Your Mind
- Shape Up Your Reading (Behavior, Art Skills, Body, Mind)
- "Let's Get Physical!"
- Feel Sharp, Be Sharp—Read!
- Reading IS NOT Hazardous to Your Health
- Read for the Fun of It

ADDITIONAL IDEAS

"Kid"

- Use alone as shown or add more "kids"
- Hinged kids provide creative positioning
- Use face and hands only as a peekover
- Use any of our "kids" to vary facial expressions, hairstyles, or accessories

SUGGESTED USES

- Curriculum, especially Physical Education
- Library/Office
- Clubs/Organizations
- Guidance/Counselor

UPPER LEGS

UPPER ARM

TORSO

LOWER LEGS

LOWER ARM

FEET: SIDE   FRONT

READING
Football Player

SPECIAL EFFECTS

Player

- Construction paper, poster board, foamcore, kraft paper, freezer paper, oaktag, plywood, upson board
- Use brass fasteners for movable joints with the following lightweight materials: paper, foamcore, or poster board
- Use bolts to fasten joints with the following heavier materials: plywood and upson board

Books

- Construction paper, poster board, oaktag, actual book jackets, wrapping paper, gift box cardboard, actual gift boxes, fabric, felt

COLOR SUGGESTIONS

- School, team, or club colors

SLOGANS

- Pile It On
- No Penalty for Reading
- Exercise Your Mind
- Reading Is a Life-Time Sport
- Super Stars
- We're on Your Reading Team

- Kick Off the Season with a Book
- Kick Off with a Book
- What a Catch!

ADDITIONAL IDEAS

Books

- Three-dimensional—stack gift boxes covered with wrapping paper, book jackets, or book covers
- Use book spines as display areas

Football player

- Place school mascot, logo, monogram on helmet or sleeve
- Substitute books with school materials and supplies (computer disks, cassettes, CDs, tools, etc.), sports equipment, etc.
- Use any of the "kids" to vary facial expressions and body positions

SUGGESTED USES

- Curriculum
- Library/Office/Cafeteria
- Sports/ Pep Club
- Clubs/Organizations
- Church Activities

READING
Ice Cream "Scoops"

SPECIAL EFFECTS

Ice cream

- Construction paper, kraft paper, colored foils, oaktag, poster board, fabric, felt, foamcore, plastic bags

Cone

- Construction paper, kraft paper, poster board, fabric, felt, burlap

Bowl

- Plastic container, aluminum foil, colored cellophane, colored foils

COLOR SUGGESTIONS

- Any color, metallics

SLOGANS

- Some Cool Ideas
- Get the Scoop
- It's Cool
- Join the "Cool" Team
- A Cool Collection
- A Sweet Alliance
- It's Cool to Stand United

- Sweets for the Sweet
- A New "Scoop" of Students (Subjects, Ideas, Topics)
- Piled High

ADDITIONAL IDEAS

Ice cream

- Stack additional scoops of ice cream to fill display needs
- Fill scoops with book titles, teaching materials, student works, etc.

Cone

- Texture cone with marker outlines or paint square designs for waffle effect
- Tea-stain fabric or felt for subtle shades of brown

Letters

- See **Lettering "How-To's"** (pp. 220–29)

SUGGESTED USES

- Curriculum
- Library/Office/Cafeteria
- Clubs/Organizations
- Church Activities

READING
Searching

SPECIAL EFFECTS

"Kid"

- Construction paper, kraft paper, poster board, fabric, felt, actual clothing, wrapping paper, wallpaper

Hunter

- Construction paper, kraft paper, fabric, poster board, felt, wrapping paper, wallpaper

Sherlock Holmes

- Construction paper, kraft paper, fabric, poster board, freezer paper, black garbage bag

Magnifying glass

- Transparency film, clear plastic wrap, foil, waxpaper, cellophane

COLOR SUGGESTIONS

"Kid"/Hunter

- Camouflage, fluorescent orange, greens, browns, tan, black, bright red

SLOGANS

- Start the Search
- Quit Snooping Around
- Can't Find the Answers? Get a Head Start With . . .
- Explore Your Future
- Investigate

- Hunting for a (Career, Good Book, Hobby, etc.)
- Look Closely
- On the Trail of a Good Book
- Track Down a Good Book
- Escape with a Book
- Strange and Unusual
- Booked for Murder
- Criminally Different

ADDITIONAL IDEAS

"Kid"

- For complete body, use any of our hinged "kids" and dress appropriately

Hunter

- Simplify by using only face and hands
- Eliminate the body and substitute with grass pattern or use natural materials such as: tall cattails, grasses, twigs, leaves, etc.

Sherlock Holmes

- Outline and fill with tempera paint or marker
- For a simple design use magnifying glass alone

SUGGESTED USES

- Curriculum
- Clubs/Organizations
- Library/Office
- Church Activities

READING
Grips

SPECIAL EFFECTS

Hands

- Construction paper, poster board, kraft paper, felt

Bat/Ball

- Construction paper, poster board, kraft paper, felt, contact paper, leatherlike material

Wrapping

- Gauze, ace bandage, athletic tape, torn fabric strips

COLOR SUGGESTIONS

- Hands—skin tones
- Ball/Bat—school colors, actual colors
- Baseball diamond—green and white, school colors

SLOGANS

- (Any subject) Is a Snap
- Put Your Hands on a Good Book
- Hand Off to Your Future
- Get a Grip on (Study) Skills
- Grab the Chance to . . .
- Hold Onto . . .
- Seize the Moment
- Get Control of Your . . .
- Embrace Knowledge
- Grab the Spirit
- It's Winsome!
- Don't Strike Out
- Pursue a Career

ADDITIONAL IDEAS

Baseball

- Substitute bat with other appropriate item such as: yardstick, paint brush, mixing spoon, color guard flag
- Vary the size and placement of the baseball diamond to create a display area

Football

- Vary the size to create a display area
- Substitute football with student works, teaching materials, slogans, etc.

SUGGESTED USES

- Seasonal
- Curriculum
- Library/Office
- Clubs/Organizations
- Sports/Pep Club

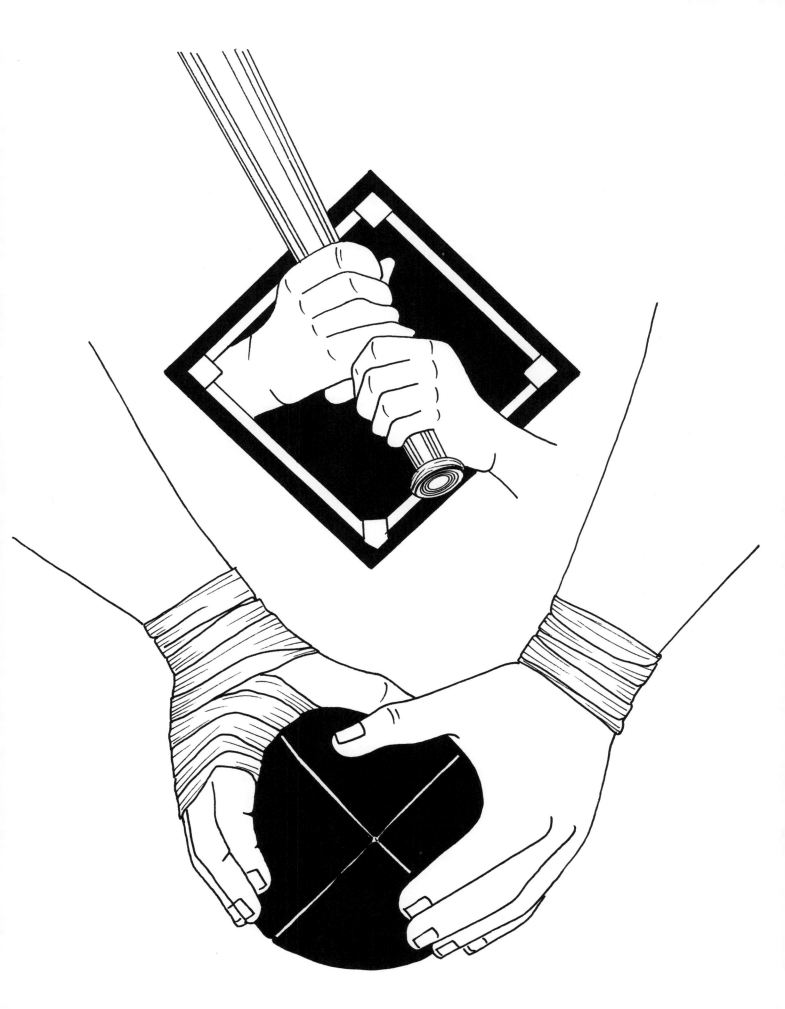

READING
Referee

SPECIAL EFFECTS

Referees

- Construction paper, poster board, kraft paper, freezer paper, oaktag, foamcore, fabric

COLOR SUGGESTIONS

- Black and white

SLOGANS

- Take Time Out to (Read, Practice, Study)
- Touchdown at . . . (the Library)
- Keep (Stay) on Top of the Action
- Time Out for . . .
- Score on . . .
- Score High!
- Bring Home a Winner
- We're on Your Team
- Everyone Wins at the Library (Cafeteria, Office, Class)
- Touchdown with a Book

- Our Goals for the Year
- It's All in the Game

ADDITIONAL IDEAS

Time-out

- Size arms to frame a display area

Touchdown

- Lengthen arms to fit a display area

Referee

- Size to frame a display area, door frame, door, window

SUGGESTED USES

- Curriculum
- Library/Office/Cafeteria
- Sports/Pep Club
- Clubs/Organizations
- Church Activities
- Back-to-school
- Guidance/Counselor

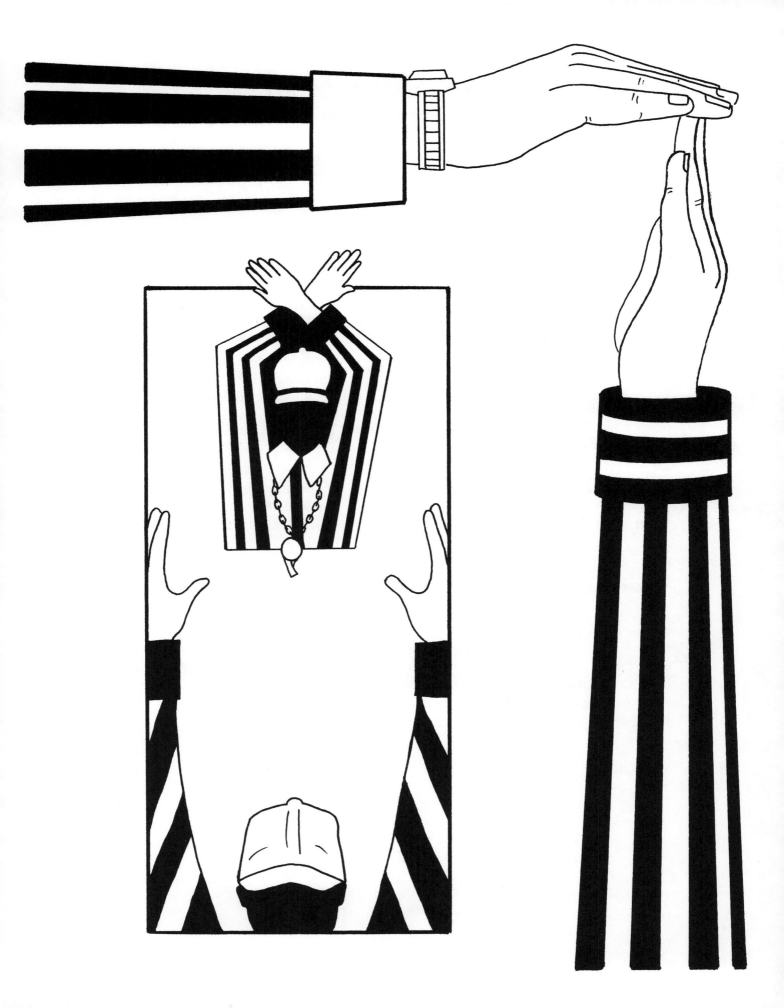

ENVIRONMENT/ECOLOGY
Save the Earth

SPECIAL EFFECTS

Hands

- Construction paper, felt, poster board, foam-core, cardboard, oaktag

Earth

- Construction paper, poster board, crumpled brown paper bag sponged with paint, Frisbee under paper for three-dimensional effect

Ocean

- Blue cellophane, blue foil, or blue cellophane over aluminum foil

Seedling

- Twig with paper leaves or flowers, silk flowers and leaves, construction paper

COLOR SUGGESTIONS

Leaves

- Variegated green

Seed

- Brown, tan, white, cream

Earth

- Blue water, green and brown continents
- Photo montage of trees, flowers, plants
- Wrapping paper (jungle, flower, foliage)

Hand

- Skin tones

SLOGANS

- Preserve the Earth
- Hold Onto the Environment
- Love the Earth
- Save the Earth
- Show Your Support
- Hold On!
- Let There Be Peace
- "We've Got the Whole World in Our Hands"
- Our Earth—Take Care of It
- Earth Belongs to Everyone

ADDITIONAL IDEAS

Hands

- Different color hands (multicultural) passing the earth to each other
- An adult hand passing the earth to a child's hand
- Hand holding the earth—cut hand along dotted line and insert earth
- Hand holding the seedling—place on whole hand

Earth

- International flags can circle the earth

SUGGESTED USES

- Curriculum, especially Science or Social Studies
- Earth Day/Arbor Day
- Multicultural—foreign-exchange programs
- Generational use—from adult to child

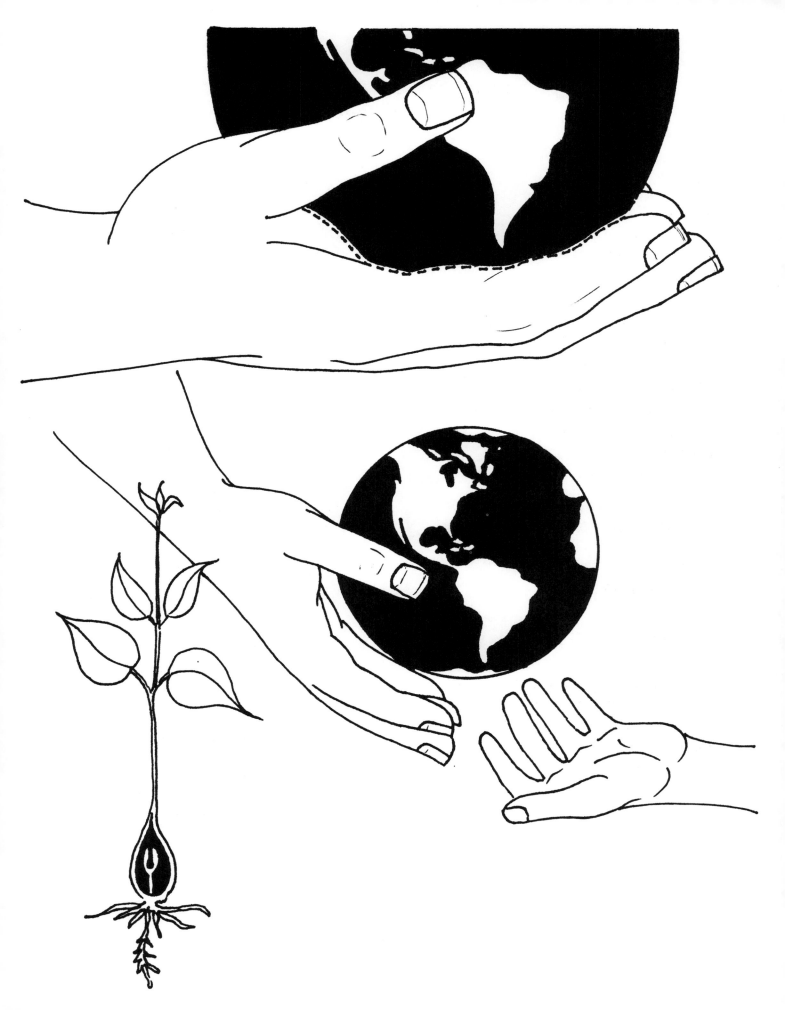

ENVIRONMENT/ECOLOGY
Hugging, Part 1

SPECIAL EFFECTS

Hearts

- Construction paper, foil, fabric, felt, magazine or newspaper pages, greeting cards, cellophane, book jackets
- Decorate with lace, doilies, rickrack

Hair

- Construction paper, felt, burlap, yarn

Earth

- See **Hugging Part 2** (pp. 130–31)

"Kid"

- Construction paper, foamcore, cardboard, poster board

COLOR SUGGESTIONS

- Hearts—red, pink, white
- Hair—brown, yellow, black, tan, orange, red, white
- Face—skin tones

SLOGANS

- Welcome to Our World
- Hug the Earth (Book or any object)
- Give a Hug
- Life Is So Sweet
- Love the Earth/World
- It's a Small, Small World

ADDITIONAL IDEAS

"Kid"

- Remove earth pattern and substitute with a large heart, book jacket, teaching supplies, or other object
- Change face from girl to boy
- Use only face and hearts

Hearts

- Make from magazine pages featuring relevant issues: peace—people together, people hugging; environment—green foliage, flowers, fruits, or vegetables
- Mix different materials or colors. Place red heart behind photo cutout. Mix solid hearts with picture hearts

SUGGESTED IDEAS

- Curriculum, Especially Science and Social Studies
- Earth Day/Arbor Day
- Valentine's Day
- Open House
- Nutrition/Health
- Foreign Relations/International Exchange Program
- Church Activities

ENVIRONMENT/ECOLOGY
Hugging, Part 2

SPECIAL EFFECTS

Earth

- Construction paper, kraft paper, or crumpled brown paper bag sponged with paint, Frisbee under paper for three-dimensional effect

"Kid"

- Construction paper, foamcore, cardboard, poster board, plywood, upson board, oaktag
- Fabric glued to any of the above materials
- Use brass fasteners for movable joints with the following lightweight materials: paper, foamcore, or poster board
- Use bolts to fasten joints with the following heavier materials: plywood or upson board

Hair

- Construction paper, felt, burlap, yarn

COLOR SUGGESTIONS

- Face—skin tones
- Clothing—denim, khaki, tan, school colors
- Shirt—red/white/blue

SLOGANS

- Sharing and Caring for the Earth
- Love the Earth/World
- Love Each Other
- "It's a Small, Small World"
- Hug the Earth (or other objects)
- Care for the Earth . . . Pass It On
- Love One Another—Let's Be Friends!
- Hug One Another—Care for Each Other

ADDITIONAL IDEAS

"Kid"

- Change face to female
- Reverse figure pattern and place one on each side of the earth
- Hug objects other than the earth
- Hug each other

Face

- For additional faces, see **Multicultural** (pp. 162–185) and **Patterns** (pp. 186–87)

SUGGESTED USES

- Curriculum, especially Science and Social Studies
- Earth Day/Arbor Day
- Foreign Relations/International Foreign Exchange Program
- Open House
- Library/Office/Cafeteria
- Church Activities
- Clubs/Organizations

ENVIRONMENT/ECOLOGY
Gardening

SPECIAL EFFECTS

Gloves

- Actual gloves, felt, fabric

Seed packets

- Construction paper, actual seed packets

Rake

- Additional rake pattern from **Fall/Thanksgiving** (pp. 36–37)

Tools

- Construction paper, aluminum or color foil, poster board, foamcore, cardboard, actual tools

Handles

- Woodgrain contact paper over paper or poster board patterns

COLOR SUGGESTIONS

- Actual colors

SLOGANS

- Care for the Earth
- A Garden of Ideas
- Fresh from the Garden
- Read Before You Plant
- Harvest Your Plants (Thoughts, Talents, Skills)
- How Does Your Garden Grow?
- Where Do We Grow from Here? (graduation)
- Take a Pick of the New Crop
- Bloom With a Book
- Pick a Good Book

ADDITIONAL IDEAS

Seed packets

- Replace with student works, photos, etc.

Wheelbarrow

- Fill with student works
- Tip over with materials spilling out

Basket

- Additional pattern in **Fall/Thanksgiving** (pp. 36–37)

SUGGESTED USES

- Seasonal
- Environmental/Ecology/Biology classes
- Arbor Day
- Gardening season
- Nutrition/Food classes
- Community Service Work

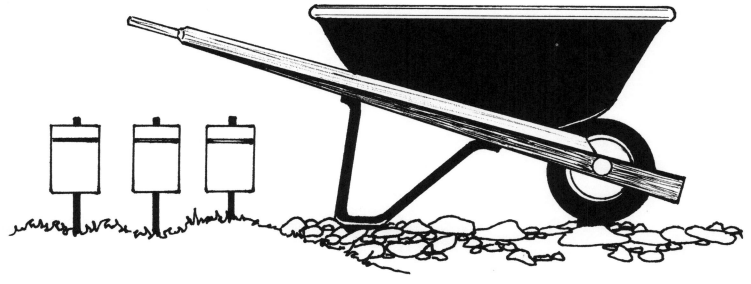

ENVIRONMENT/ECOLOGY
Piggy Bank

SPECIAL EFFECTS

Bank

- Construction paper, poster board, foamcore, felt, wrapping paper, magazine pages, maps

Coins

- Construction paper, aluminum/colored foils, cardboard, poster board, foamcore, maps, earth forms

Letters

- See **Lettering "How-To's"** (pp. 220–29)

COLOR SUGGESTIONS

- Bank—pink, white, tan, brown, black, earth tone

SLOGANS

- Save the Earth
- Save for Tomorrow
- Preserve/Conserve the Earth
- Save for the Future
- "A Penny Saved Is a Penny Earned"
- You Can Bank on It!
- Don't Bankrupt the Earth—Conserve
- Wet Your Appetite (use water drops instead of coins)

ADDITIONAL IDEAS

Coins

- Use as the center of flowers (see **Patterns,** pp. 21–13)
- Substitute with leaves, flowers, seeds, fruit, vegetables, blood drops, globe, maps, book jackets, water drops

Bank

- Montage of flags from different nations
- Montage of environmental topics
- Substitute piggy bank with a slotted earth-shaped bank

SUGGESTED USES

- Blood Drive—replace coins with blood drops
- Nutrition or Consumer Services
- College/Career Day—financial aid for higher education
- Library
- Clubs/Organizations
- Church Activities
- Curriculum, Especially Science and Social Studies

PATRIOTISM
Uncle Sam

SPECIAL EFFECTS

Hat

- Construction paper, poster board, fabric, felt, foil, actual hat made of Styrofoam or pressed paper

Face/Hand

- Construction paper, oaktag, poster board, foamcore, kraft paper

Hair

- Construction paper, poster board, fabric, felt, cotton, yarn, heavy cording, white mop

Clothing

- Construction paper, poster board, fabric, felt, wrapping paper

COLOR SUGGESTIONS

- Hat, accessories, lettering—red, white and blue
- Coat—black, blue, navy

SLOGANS

- Yankee Doodle Dandy!
- I Want You:
  To Just Say No
  To Schedule for Next Year
  To Get Heart Smart
  To Get "Art" Smart (any topic)
- Knowledge Is Power (Biographies)
- Men of Destiny (Biographies)
- Work We're Proud Of!
- Profiles in Courage (Biographies)
- The People, Yes

ADDITIONAL IDEAS

Face/Hand

- Use simplified version to frame existing bulletin board display area, door, window, cabinet or wall
- Shade with pastels, colored pencils, crayons
- Use as a peekover

Eyebrows and beard

- The same color and material as hair
- Three-dimensional effect—make a second hand and raise it from the surface by gluing a piece of sponge to the back

SUGGESTED USES

- Curriculum, especially Nutrition, Drug Awareness, Health and Safety, Social Studies
- American Education Week
- Library/Office/Cafeteria
- Club/Church organizations
- Back-to-School
- Seasonal—Fourth of July decorations and posters
- Presidential/school elections
- Military display

PATRIOTISM
Politics

SPECIAL EFFECTS

Hats

- Construction paper, poster board, fabric, felt, foil, actual hat made of Styrofoam or pressed paper

Drapes

- Sheets, tissue paper, crepe paper, or actual curtains
- Fabric materials such as felt, velvet, or silk lining

Figures

- Construction paper, poster board, kraft paper, fabric, gift box cardboard, felt

COLOR SUGGESTIONS

- Red, white, or blue

SLOGANS

- Back in the Ring (symbols represents each political party)
- Salute to America's Finest
- The American Way
- So Proudly We Hail
- Vote for These (Books, Reports, Photos, etc.)
- Celebrating Our Freedom to Read (to Learn, to Think)
- Only in America
- Both Our Houses
- A Political Platform
- Spotlight on . . .

ADDITIONAL IDEAS

Empty top hat

- Celebrate a presidential birthday or governmental event by filling the hat with materials such as: banners, slogans, confetti, balloons, tissue paper, streamers, wrapped gifts, symbolic items, etc.

Display area

- Frame with draped fabric

SUGGESTED USES

- Curriculum
- Library/Office/Cafeteria
- American Education Week
- Presidential election, birthdays
- Military display
- Seasonal—Fourth of July decorations, posters
- School/Club elections

PATRIOTISM
American Education Week

SPECIAL EFFECTS

U.S.A.

- Actual map, kraft paper, freezer paper, construction paper, poster board, oaktag

State

- Construction paper, poster board, foamcore, metallic paper, contact paper

COLOR SUGGESTIONS

- U.S.A.—cream, light gray, white, beige, yellow, neutrals
- State—white outlined in state colors, or red, white and blue
- Lettering—red, white, blue

SLOGANS

- Celebrate the Spirit of Success
- "We Proudly Hail . . ."
- Celebrate! A Salute to . . .
- The Pride of America
- Education Can Unite Us

ADDITIONAL IDEAS

- Highlight an individual state
- See **Patterns** (pp. 208–9)

Three-dimensional effect

- Cut out and raise state from the surface by gluing a piece of sponge to the back

Hometown location

- Mark with a schoolhouse, school symbol, logo, flag, star, etc. (see **Back-to-School,** pp. 14–15)

Letters

- To create striped effect, paint or paste colored strips to top of paper before cutting out a letter
- See **Lettering "How-To's"** (pp. 220–29)

SUGGESTED USES

- Curriculum
- Library/Office/Cafeteria
- American Education Week
- Presidential elections, birthdays
- Seasonal—Fourth of July decorations and posters
- Military display

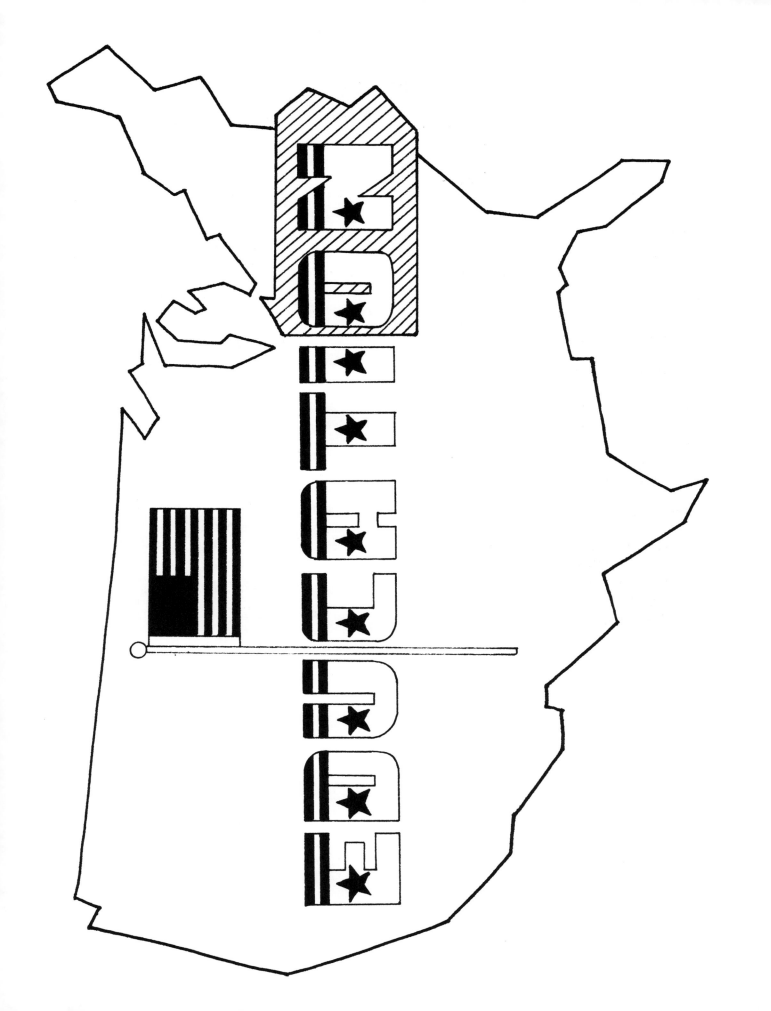

SOCIAL ISSUES
AIDS

SPECIAL EFFECTS

Time Bomb

- Construction paper, poster board, foamcore, kraft paper, contact paper, felt, wrapping paper, vinyl, black garbage bag

Wick

- Pipe cleaner, string with unraveled ends, foil

Fluids

- Construction paper, poster board, foil, cellophane, cellophane rubber cemented to aluminum foil, clear contact paper, plastic wrap, plastic bottle, transparency film, wax paper

Lettering

- Construction paper, poster board, foamcore, felt, fabric, wrapping paper, kraft paper, freezer paper, contact paper

COLOR SUGGESTIONS

- Time bomb—black, gray, dull green, brown
- Fluids—pastels, metallic, semitranslucent
- Lettering—bright bold colors: red, orange, yellow, fluorescent

SLOGANS

Time bomb

- The Time Bomb
- AIDS—Don't Die of Ignorance
- Gay or Straight, Male or Female, Anyone Can Get AIDS
- How You Won't Get AIDS
- Fight the Fear with Facts
- Concerned—Not Afraid
- AIDS—A Deadly Force
- Why Play With Danger?
- Getting AIDS

Liquids

- The Deadly Liquids
- AIDS—It Dissolves Life
- Liquidate AIDS
- "Dissoluble Solutions"
- "It Can't Happen to Me!"

ADDITIONAL IDEAS

Time bomb—three-dimensional

- Cover a Frisbee, half of rubber/beach ball, or garbage can lid with any of the suggested materials

Lettering

- Size letters to fill the entire display area (see **Lettering "How-To's"** (pp. 220–29)
- Cover either background area or letters with a montage of magazine/newspaper articles/photos on AIDS
- Cut two sets of letters in contrasting colors and stagger to create a shadow effect

Three-dimensional effect

- Make a second letter and raise it from the surface by gluing pieces of sponge to the back

Fluids

- Add extra drops and label with the four deadly liquids: semen, saliva, blood, urine
- Add skulls/skeletons (see **Halloween,** pp. 24–26 and **Multicultural,** pp. 182–83)

SUGGESTED USES

- Curriculum, especially Health, Science, Sociology
- Library/Office/Cafeteria
- Clubs/Organizations
- Guidance/Counselor
- Church Activities

SOCIAL ISSUES
Playing Cards/Hang-ups

SPECIAL EFFECTS

Playing cards

- Construction paper, poster board, foamcore, kraft paper, place mats, actual cards

Hang-ups

- Rope—Actual cording, yarn, ribbon, chain
- Hangers—Wire, pipe cleaners, poster board cut-outs

COLOR SUGGESTIONS

- Cards—black, white, red
- Hang-Ups—bright, bold colors

SLOGANS

Playing Cards

- Play (It) Straight
- Play Fair
- Fair Play
- Playing with Math (any subject)
- Decisions
- Books Fit for a King (Queen)
- Don't Gamble (Your Life Away)

Hang-ups

- Don't Get Hooked On . . .
- Hang in There
- Hang Up Your Problems. Get Counseling!
- Suspend Your Problems
- Hold That Line
- What's Your Line?

ADDITIONAL IDEAS

Playing cards

- Color face cards with marker, poster paint, crayons

Hang-ups

- Use actual items such as: hangers, clothes-pins, clips

SUGGESTED USES

- Curriculum
- Guidance/Counselor
- Library/Office/Cafeteria
- Clubs/Organizations
- Church Activities

HANG-UPS

FOOD BEER DRUGS DRINKING SEX

SOCIAL ISSUES
Peer Problems

SPECIAL EFFECTS

Figures

- Construction paper, typing or computer paper, kraft paper, wrapping paper, freezer paper, fabric, contact paper

Squares of items

- Newspaper/magazine articles, cut photos from advertisements or brochures, actual items, construction paper, poster board, kraft paper

COLOR SUGGESTIONS

- Figures—neutral, blue, grays, white
- Squares—bright, bold, actual colors

SLOGANS

- You Are What Your Friends Are
- You Are Judged by the Company You Keep
- Don't Fall Into a Bad Habit

- "United We Stand, Divided We Fall"
- Peers, Pals, and Problems
- Where Are You Going?

ADDITIONAL IDEAS

Figures

- Make individually or as a chain of paper dolls by folding and cutting lightweight paper. See half-pattern in figure at right of art

Squares of items

- Make the square designs empty. Have students provide sketches,pictures,articles,or photos that represent personal problems.

SUGGESTED USES

- Curriculum, especially Health
- Library/Office/Cafeteria
- Clubs/Organizations
- Guidance/Counselor
- Church Activities

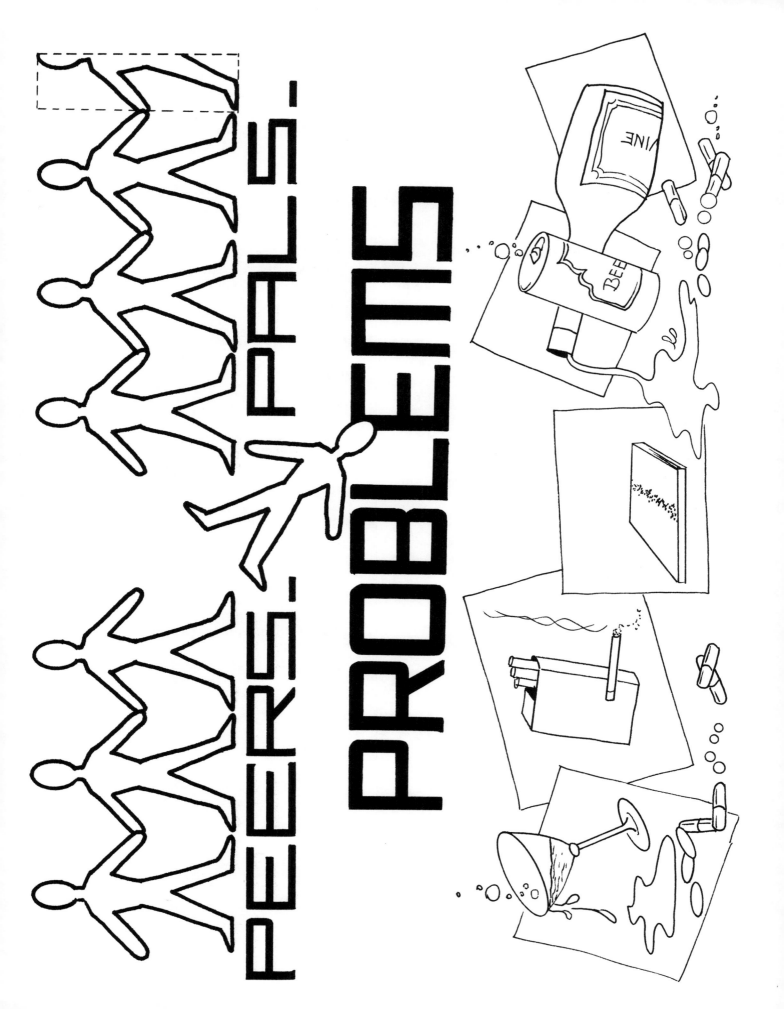

SOCIAL ISSUES
Suicide

SPECIAL EFFECTS

Figures

- Drawing paper, construction paper, poster board, oaktag, gift box cardboard
- Use brass fasteners for movable joints with the following lightweight materials: paper, poster board, and gift-box cardboard

COLOR SUGGESTIONS

- Neutrals, black and white, light grays or blues

SLOGANS

- Too Young to Die
- Suicide Is Preventable
- Show That You Care
- Be a Good Listener
- Choose to Live
- Get Help
- Look at the Statistics
- Be a Buddy
- Someone Cares
- Don't Be Confused
- You Don't Have to Be Alone
- Note: Use current statistics on suicide as a part of a slogan. The warning signs of suicide (depression, drop in grades, change in habits, pressure to succeed, etc.) can become part of the display by printing them inside caption balloons.

ADDITIONAL IDEAS

Figures

- Use figures alone or in groups
- Any position is possible. Experiment for emotional impact
- Add skulls/skeletons to the design (see **Halloween,** pp. 24–26 and **Multicultural,** pp. 182–83)

SUGGESTED USES

- Curriculum
- Guidance/Counselor
- Library/Office
- Church Activities
- Clubs/Organizations

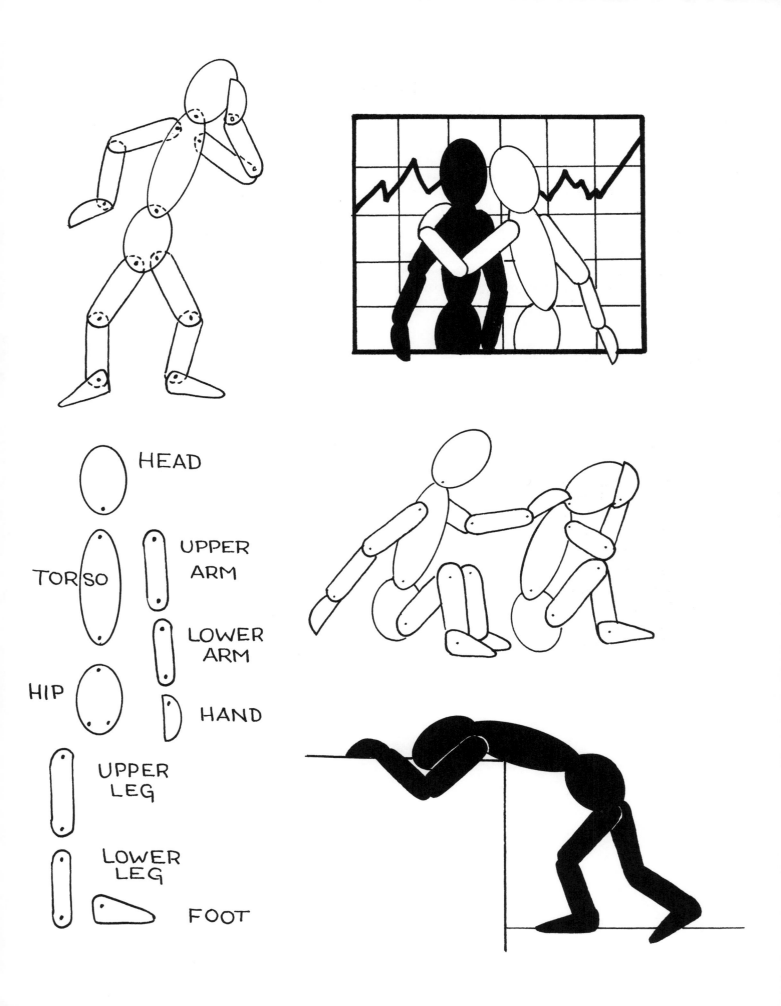

HEAD

TORSO

UPPER
ARM

LOWER
ARM

HIP

HAND

UPPER
LEG

LOWER
LEG

FOOT

SOCIAL ISSUES
Drugs/Alcohol

SPECIAL EFFECTS

Pills/Bottle

- Construction paper, poster board, foamcore
- Cover with shiny material such as: clear contact paper, plastic wrap, transparency film, plastic wrap

Figures

- Drawing paper, construction paper, poster board, oaktag, gift box cardboard
- Use brass fasteners for movable joints with the following lightweight materials: paper, poster board, and gift box cardboard

Chains/Lock

- Foil, metallic paper, construction paper, poster board, actual chain and lock

COLOR SUGGESTIONS

- Figures—bright colors: red, yellow, orange, light grays and blues, browns, black
- Chains/Lock—dark colors: grays, black, metallics
- Pills—bright colors

SLOGANS

- Are You Trapped?
- Don't Get Trapped in a Bad Habit
- Locked In?
- Locked In!
- Free Yourself
- Who Am I?
- Where Am I Going?

ADDITIONAL IDEAS

Figures

- Vary position to stand, sit, carry, hold, climb
- Illustrate different emotions such as depression, loneliness, and stress through body language

Chain

- Wrap chain around pills

SUGGESTED USES

- Curriculum, especially Health and Sociology
- Guidance/Counselor
- Library/Office/Cafeteria
- Clubs/Organizations
- Church Activities

SOCIAL ISSUES
Street Violence/Handgun

SPECIAL EFFECTS

Gun

- Construction paper, poster board, foamcore, foils, tooling foil, metallic spray paint

Hand

- Construction paper, poster board, kraft paper, oaktag

Flame

- Cellophane, foil, construction paper, colored cellophane rubber cemented to foil, crayon slivers ironed and melted between wax paper

COLOR SUGGESTIONS

- Gun—metallics, gray, black
- Hand—white, gray, skin tones
- Letters—bright bold colors: red, orange, yellow, fluorescent

SLOGANS

- Can the Cycle Be Stopped?
- When Kids Kill

- Is Your Neighborhood Safe?
- Fight Fear with Facts
- Fatal and Final
- Standing Up to Violence
- Stop the Violence
- Take Aim Against Violence
- Note: Use current statistics on violence as part of a slogan

ADDITIONAL IDEAS

Guns

- To create the effect of the gun firing use flour, glitter, red/orange cellophane, colored chalk
- Three-dimensional effect—raise design from surface by gluing a piece of sponge to the back

SUGGESTED USES

- Curriculum
- Library/Office/Cafeteria
- Clubs/Organizations
- Church Activities
- Guidance/Counselor

SOCIAL ISSUES
School Violence/Target

SPECIAL EFFECTS

School

- Construction paper, poster board, kraft paper, computer paper

Target site

- Plastic wrap, cellophane, waxpaper, clear contact paper, transparency film

Crosshairs

- Strips of thin paper or cardboard, yarn, rope, pipe cleaners, straws, dowel rods, cording, wire, black marker

COLOR SUGGESTIONS

- Lettering/crosshairs—bold colors: black, red, orange, yellow
- School—neutral, gray
- Actual colors: blue sky, green grass, gray building

SLOGANS

- Is Your School Safe?
- The Unknown Figures and Facts
- Take Aim! Fight Back!
- Stop! Don't Shoot!
- Violence in Our Schools
- Sobering Statistics
- When Kids Kill
- Standing Up to Violence
- Note: Use current statistics on violence as a part of the slogan

ADDITIONAL IDEAS

Target—Bullet Holes

- Punch holes from reverse side to create a three-dimensional effect
- Back holes with contrasting colored paper

Schoolhouse

- See **Back-to-School** (p. 15) for additional school design
- Simple cut paper, silhouette, paint, or marker outline

SUGGESTED USES

- Curriculum
- Library/Office/Cafeteria
- Clubs/Organizations
- Church Activities
- Guidance/Counselor

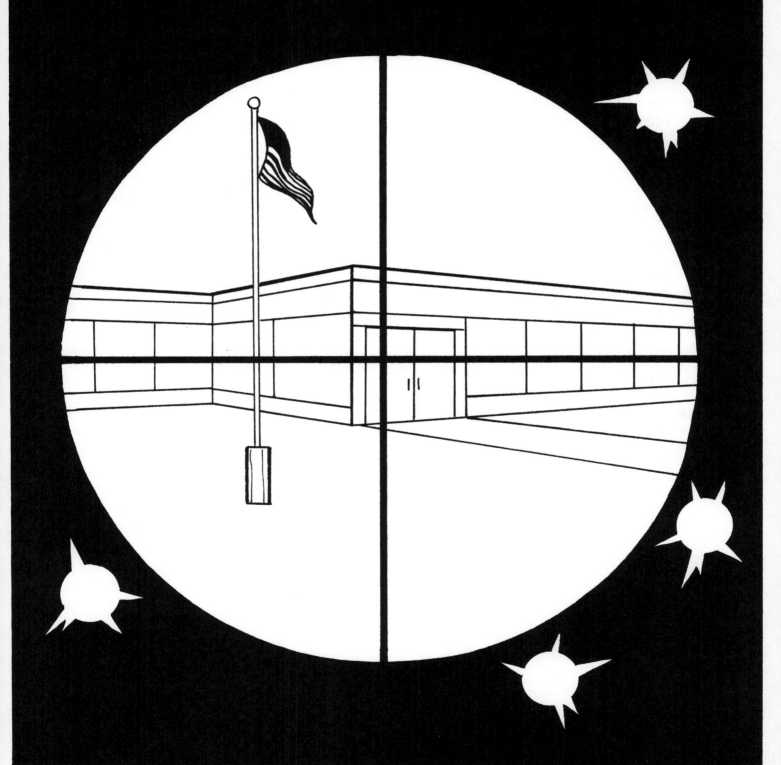

SOCIAL ISSUES
School Violence/Glasses

SPECIAL EFFECTS

Broken glasses

- Construction paper, poster board, kraft paper, oaktag, foils, actual glasses (old)

Lenses

- Glass, Plexiglass, plastic bottle, plastic wrap, cellophane, transparency film, waxpaper, clear contact paper, mirror

COLOR SUGGESTIONS

- School colors
- Black and white
- Bright bold colors: red, orange, yellow, fluorescent

SLOGANS

- Shattering Statistics
- Violent Hallways
- Is Your School Safe?
- The Unknown Figures
- Violence in our Schools
- Standing Up to Violence
- Sobering Statistics
- Note: Use current statistics on violence as a part of a slogan

ADDITIONAL IDEAS

Broken glasses

- Break actual pair of eyeglasses
- Create broken effect with magic marker

SUGGESTED USES

- Curriculum
- Office/Library/Cafeteria
- Clubs/Organizations
- Guidance/Counselor
- Church Activities

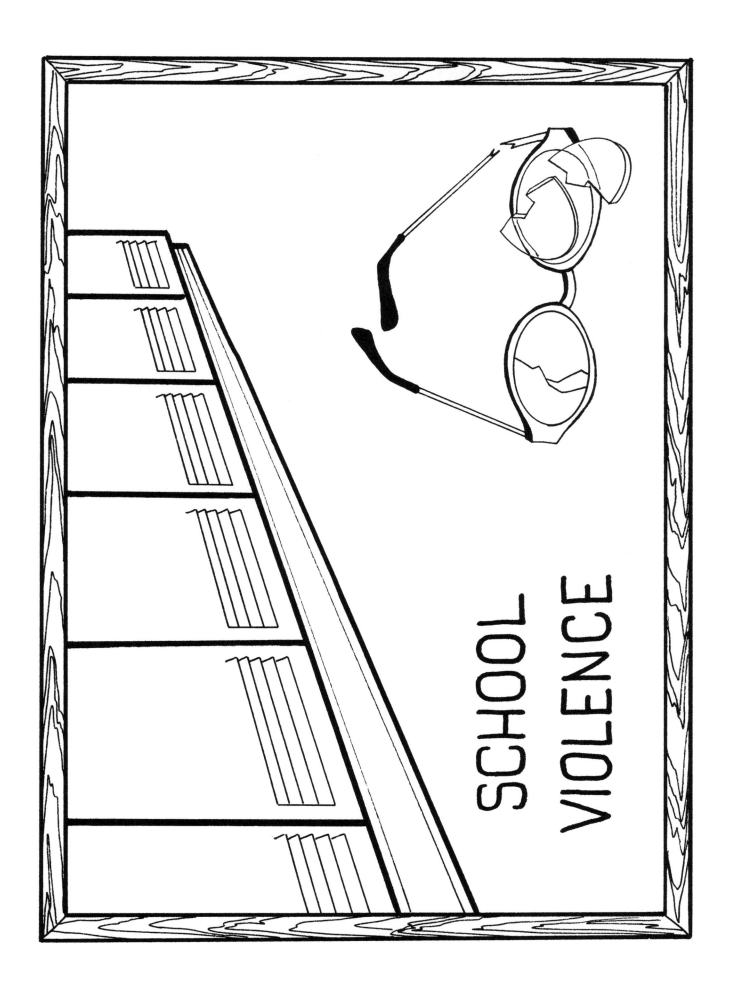

SCHOOL
VIOLENCE

SOCIAL ISSUES
Ethnic

SPECIAL EFFECTS

Black/White

- Construction paper, poster board, foamcore, gift box cardboard, kraft paper, freezer paper

Globe

- Actual map (cut), construction paper, freezer paper

Controversy

- Construction paper, poster board, contact paper, foamcore, kraft paper, gift box cardboard, freezer paper

COLOR SUGGESTIONS

Black/White

- Faces—black, white, skin tones
- Eyes—bright, bold colors, actual map colors
- Lettering—bold, bright colors

Controversy

- Faces—black, white, skin-tones
- Lettering—bold, bright colors

SLOGANS

- Africa, Then/Now—The Face of Time
- Black/White
- Hate and Crime
- Controversy
- Prejudice
- Different yet the Same

ADDITIONAL IDEAS

Black/White

- Use world globe for eye
- Highlight a particular country or continent
- Additional heads can represent the many races and cultures of the world

Controversy—three-dimensional hanging display

- Cut two sheets to size needed.
- Make the designs front and back on both sheets.
- Cut slots, assemble and hang.

Background

- Montage of related news items, magazines, photographs

SUGGESTED USES

- Curriculum, especially Social Studies
- Library/Office/Cafeteria
- Clubs/Organizations
- Guidance/Counselor
- Church Activities

BLACK WHITE

CUT SLOTS

ASSEMBLE & HANG

←CONTROVERSY→

MULTICULTURAL
Hanukkah/Star of David

SPECIAL EFFECTS

Star

- Construction paper, kraft paper, poster board, foamcore, foil, felt, fabric, ribbons, trims, braids, crepe paper, wrapping paper, contact paper, gift box cardboard

Letters

- Construction paper, magazine pages, foil, holiday greeting cards, wrapping paper

COLOR SUGGESTIONS

- Metallics
- Primary colors

SLOGAN

- The Star of David
- Interwoven Faith

- Shield of David
- God Is Everywhere
- The Miracle of Freedom

ADDITIONAL IDEAS

Star

- Overlap two solid equilateral triangles
- Interweave triangles with hollow centers

Lettering

- See **Lettering "How-To's"** (pp. 220–29)

SUGGESTED USES

- Curriculum
- Seasonal
- Synagogue/Church Activities
- Clubs/Organizations
- Library/Office/Cafeteria

HAPPY HANUKKAH

MULTICULTURAL
Hanukkah/Menorah

SPECIAL EFFECTS

Candles

- Construction paper, kraft paper, poster board, fabric, foil, wrapping or freezer paper, gift box cardboard

Candleholder/Menorah

- Construction paper, poster board, kraft paper, foamcore, cardboard, foil over poster board, tooling foil, spray painted cardboard

Flames

- Cellophane, foil, construction paper, colored cellophane rubber cemented to foil, crayon slivers ironed and melted between wax papers

COLOR SUGGESTIONS

- Candleholder—metallics

SLOGANS

- A Festival of Lights
- I See the Light
- It Just Dawned on Me
- ". . . In the Dark"
- "Hope Is a Heritage That Burns Brightly Even Through the Darkest Night"
- The Power of Light
- "Kindle the Light"

- In Times of Darkness or Uncertainty, Love and Light Triumph . . . Faith Prevails

ADDITIONAL IDEAS

Three-dimensional candles

- Cardboard tubing (toilet tissue, paper towel, wrapping paper, etc.) covered with the above materials
- Drip wax crayons over upper edge of tubing

Three-dimensional candleholder

- Long, rectangular product boxes from wax paper, aluminum foil, or plastic wrap

Menorah

- Cut holes the size of cardboard tubing (candles) in top of the boxes

Base

- Milk cartons (quart, half gallon) covered with any of the above materials

Flame Stem

- Use long matchsticks, straws, thin dowel rods, or strips of cardboard. Attach flames and insert into hollow tubes.

SUGGESTED USES

- Synagogue/Church Activities
- Seasonal
- Curriculum

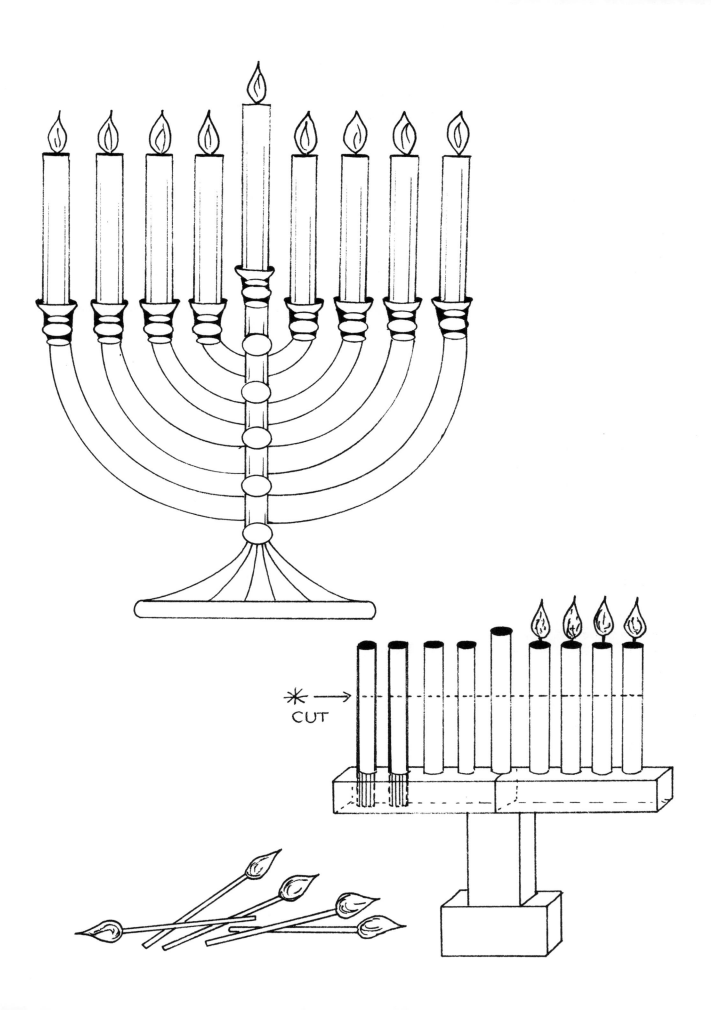

CUT

MULTICULTURAL
Hanukkah/Dreidel

SPECIAL EFFECTS

Dreidel

- Construction paper, kraft paper, cardboard, foamcore, contact paper, wrapping paper, holiday greeting cards, foils, fabric, felt, oaktag

COLOR SUGGESTIONS

- Bright festive colors
- Symbols—contrasting solid colors

SLOGANS

- A Great Miracle Happened Here
- Happy Hanukkah
- Celebrate the Miracle of Freedom

ADDITIONAL IDEAS

Three-dimensional

- Make from half pint milk or juice cartons (* see example). Cover with materials, paint with magic marker, tempera paint, or spray paint. Insert pencil/dowel rod in bottom of box for handle
- Place symbols on all four sides (cut from contact paper or use magic marker)
- Use as gift boxes or party favors by opening spout end. Fill with tissue paper and small gift
- Use as centerpiece

SUGGESTED USES

- Seasonal
- Curriculum area
- Synagogue/Church Activities
- Library/Office/Cafeteria
- Clubs/Organizations

MULTICULTURAL
Hanukkah/Child Playing

SPECIAL EFFECTS

Body

- Construction paper, poster board, foamcore, fabric, felt, gift box cardboard, plywood, upson board
- Use brass fasteners for movable joints with the following lightweight materials: paper, foamcore, or poster board
- Use bolts to fasten joints with the following heavier materials: plywood and upson board

Clothes

- Fabric, felt, construction paper, wrapping paper, wall paper
- Actual clothing

Yarmulke

- Shiny papers or materials: taffeta, lining, satin, silk

Hair

- Construction paper, felt, burlap, fun fur

COLOR SUGGESTIONS

- Holiday colors

- Yarmulke—white, metallics
- National colors: blue/white

SLOGANS

- Happy Hanukkah
- A Miracle Happened Here
- The Miracle of Freedom

ADDITIONAL IDEAS

Face

- Change to female (see **Patterns,** pp. 188–95)

Body

- Reverse figure and place one opposite the other
- See **Patterns** (pp. 188–95)

SUGGESTED USES

- Seasonal
- Curriculum
- Office/Cafeteria/Library
- Clubs/Organizations
- Church Activities

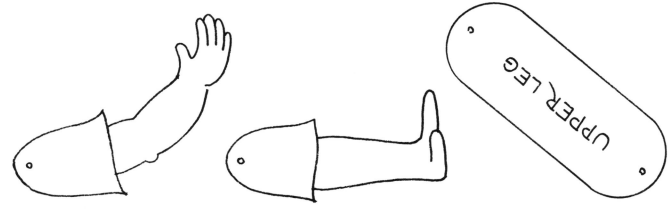

UPPER LEG

MULTICULTURAL
Kwanzaa/Kinara

SPECIAL EFFECTS

Kinara (wooden candle holder)

- Woodgrain contact paper, construction paper, foamcore, kraft paper, poster board, cardboard

Mishumaa saba (candles)

- Construction paper, poster board, foil, wrapping paper, cardboard tubing

Flame

- Cellophane, foil, construction paper, colored cellophane rubber cemented to foil, crayons slivers ironed and melted between wax paper

Borders

- Construction paper, fabric, freezer paper, wrapping paper, contact paper, kraft paper

COLOR SUGGESTIONS

- Candles—three green on right side, three red on left side, and one black in center
- Kinara—woodgrain, brown

SLOGANS

- "HARAMBEE!"
- Let's Pull Together
- Kwanzaa—First Fruits of the Harvest
- "Habari Gani?" (What's the News?)

ADDITIONAL IDEAS

- Kwanzaa is a "riddle of sevens." Patterns, borders, etc., could be in sevens

Borders

- Stenciled
- Folded and cut paper
- One design reproduced and colored
- Commercially produced
- Computerized designs

Kinara

- See **Hanukkah/Menorah** (p. 164) for three-dimensional candleholder.

SUGGESTED USES

- Curriculum
- Church Organizations
- Library/Office/Cafeteria
- Clubs/Organizations

MULTICULTURAL
Kwanzaa/Symbols

SPECIAL EFFECTS

Mazao (Fruits and vegetables)
Vibunzi (Corn)
Mkeka (Mat)
Kikombe Cha Omoja (Cup)
- Construction paper, poster board, kraft paper, wrapping paper, colored magazine pages, tissue paper, fabric, wallpaper

COLOR SUGGESTIONS

- Primary and bright colors

SLOGANS

- Seven Principles
- "The First"
- First Fruits of the Harvest

ADDITIONAL IDEAS

Corn/Vegetables/Fruits

- Make 3-dimensional by using actual produce, cornhusks and corn kernels, plastic, wooden, or stuffed fabric forms

Mat

- Brown paper bag, kraft paper, magazine covers or pages, ribbon, braids, fabric, poster board, wrapping paper, actual grass mat, printed placemat, self woven (see **Mat Directions,** pp. 174–76)

Unity cup

- Actual plastic cup, clear plastic goblet decorated with paint, marker, fabric, paper patterns.
- Use plastic containers (whipping cream, margarine, etc.) and assemble, spray paint, and decorate

Corn

- Use paper hole punch-outs and glue to cob shape

SUGGESTED USES

- Curriculum
- Seasonal
- Library/Library/Cafeteria
- Church Organization

VIBUNZI

MKEKA

MAZAO

KIKOMEE CHA
UMOJA

MULTICULTURAL
Kwanzaa/Mat (Mkeka) Directions

SPECIAL EFFECTS

- Mkekas can be woven as individual projects for display, personal use, or as a craft project.

Mat base (web)

- Heavy construction paper, poster board, oaktag, kraft paper, brown paper bags, fabrics, wood-grained contact paper (with backing left attached)

Weaving strips

- Construction paper, magazine covers and pages, kraft paper, paper bags, fabrics, felt, burlap, yarn, ribbon, veneer strips
- Natural sources for weaving are: tall grass, cattail stems and leaves, rushes, sea-oat stems and leaves, reeds, ripped corn husks, or any type of tall, thin plant

DIRECTIONS

- Select a sturdy material for the mat's base sized from 9" x 12" to 12" x 18"

- Fold in half
- Rule a line 1/2" in from open edges. This is the stopping point for all cuts
- Start at the folded edge and cut toward the ruled edge. Cuts may be straight, curved, zig-zagged, or creatively mixed
- Open mat
- Select strips of weaving materials
- Weave strips over one cut then under the next cut and repeat
- Select colors and textures for unity and variety
- Glue ends of all strips to mat base. Rubber cement for paper materials and use hot glue or tacky glue for fabric, natural materials, etc. Trim ends

HINTS TO SAVE TIME

- Use a paper cutter to cut most weaving materials. They may vary in size from 1/2" to 2" in thickness

MULTICULTURAL
Chinese New Year

SPECIAL EFFECTS

Dragon

- Construction paper, wrapping paper, magazine covers/pages, fabric, felt, kraft paper, wallpaper, tissue paper, contact paper, poster board, oaktag

Lanterns

- Construction paper, poster board, kraft paper, tissue paper, waxpaper, freezer paper, parchment, colored cellophane, plastic wrap, crepe paper

Bamboo

- Construction paper, poster board, kraft paper, foamcore, contact paper (wood grain)

Letters

- Construction paper, poster board, kraft paper, contact paper, wallpaper, wrapping paper

COLOR SUGGESTIONS

- Dragon—red, oranges, yellow, bright color
- Bamboo—greens, tans, white, cream
- Letters—red, yellow, bright, bold colors
- Lanterns—white, creams, yellow, bright, bold colors

SLOGANS

- Chinese New Year
- Good Luck and a Prosperous New Year
- "Yuan Tan"

ADDITIONAL IDEAS

Bamboo

- Create a display area by using bamboo as a frame

Lanterns

- Enlarge patterns. Cut in pairs. Staple together with white minilights sandwiched in between. String across display area

Dragon

- Cut circles or ovals for body sections and size dragon to fit display area or needs

Chinese letters

- Cut a supply of "strokes" in each of the three sizes (see top of page) and arrange as shown

SUGGESTED USES

- Curriculum
- Seasonal
- Library/Office/Cafeteria
- Clubs/Organizations
- Church Activities

MULTICULTURAL
Cinco de Mayo/Mexican Flag

SPECIAL EFFECTS

Flag
- Construction paper, poster board, contact paper, freezer paper, kraft paper, fabric, felt, nylon, large map of Mexico

Maracas
- Construction paper, poster board, wrapping paper, wallpaper, magazine covers/pages, contact paper, shelf paper

Guitar
- Construction paper, poster board, oaktag, wood-grained contact paper, kraft paper, cardboard, gift box cardboard

COLOR SUGGESTIONS

- Flag—green, white, red
- Guitar—browns, tans
- Maracas—bright, bold colors, especially reds and golds

SLOGANS

- Cinco de Mayo
- A Celebration of Independence
- The Fifth of May
- A Day of Pride
- Celebrate!
- In 1862 the French Met Their "Waterloo"

ADDITIONAL IDEAS

Flag/Background
- Actual map of Mexico, tinted with water color washes of green (neutral) and red
- Exchange guitar and maracas with other Mexincan symbols
- Mexican symbols such as: piñatas, sombreros, musical instruments, food, or flowers
- Place "kids" dressed in traditional costume alone or in groups (see **Patterns,** pp. 190–95)

SUGGESTED USES

- Curriculum
- Seasonal
- Library/Office/Cafeteria
- Clubs/Organizations
- Church Activities

CINCO DE MAYO

MULTICULTURAL
Cinco de Mayo/Piñatas/"Kid"

SPECIAL EFFECTS

"Kid"

- Construction paper, poster board, foamcore, fabric, felt, gift box cardboard, plywood, upson board, oaktag
- Use brass fasteners for movable joints with the following lightweight materials: paper, foamcore, or poster board
- Use bolts to fasten joints with the following heavier materials: plywood and upson board

Clothes

- Fabric, felt, construction paper
- Actual clothing

Hair

- Construction paper, felt, burlap, fun fur

Pinatas

- Crepe paper, tissue paper, Kleenex, light-weight fabric such as lining and nylon

COLOR SUGGESTIONS

- Red, white, green, bright, bold colors

SLOGANS

- Celebrate!

- Mexican Holidays

ADDITIONAL IDEAS

"Kid"

- Change to female
- Reverse figure
- See **Patterns** (pp. 188–95) and **Back-to-School** (pp. 6–9) for additional figures

Piñatas

- Cut any animal shape (see **Patterns,** pp. 214–19) and cover with crumpled light-weight materials such as: tissue paper, crepe paper, Kleenex, thin fabric, etc.

Three-dimensional

- Cut material in small squares, place and shape over pencil eraser, dip in glue, and apply to shape

SUGGESTED USES

- Curriculum
- Seasonal
- Library/Office/Cafeteria
- Clubs/Organizations
- Church Activities

MULTICULTURAL
Los Dias de los Muertos/Skulls/Skeletons

SPECIAL EFFECTS

Skulls/Skeleton

- Construction paper, poster board, foamcore, oaktag, gift box cardboard, plywood, upson board
- Use brass fasteners for movable joints with the following lightweight materials: paper, foamcore, or poster board
- Use bolts to fasten joints with the following heavier materials: plywood and upson board

COLOR SUGGESTIONS

- Skulls—white trimmed with yellow, orange, magenta, green, blue

SLOGANS

- The Days of the Dead
- Los Dias de los Muertos
- Celebrate!
- A Time to Remember the Dead
- El Esqueleto
- Death Is Not to Be Feared
- Death Is a Part of Life
- Remembering the Dead

ADDITIONAL IDEAS

Skeletons/Skulls

- Use our basic skull/skeleton patterns (see **Halloween,** pp. 24–26)
- Personalize with crosses, flowers, names of deceased, or any creative design
- If made life-size (child or adult), accessorize with actual clothing
- Make a freestanding centerpiece with a supporting easel. Use on top of counters, cabinets, desks, etc.
- Always smiling to lessen fear of death and to show human ironical nature

Letters

- Use bone patterns as lettering strokes (see **Lettering "How-To's,"** pp. 220–29)

SUGGESTED USES

- Curriculum
- Seasonal
- Library/Office/Cafeteria
- Clubs/Organizations
- Church Activities

LOS DIAS
DE LOS MUERTOS

MULTICULTURAL
Los Dias de los Muertos/Flowers of the Dead

SPECIAL EFFECTS

Marigoldlike flower (Cempasuchil)
Cockscomb (Mano de leon)
Nube
Gladiolus
Carnation
- Construction paper, poster board, tissue paper, wallpaper, drawing paper, wrapping paper, greeting cards, calendar photos

COLOR SUGGESTIONS

- Marigoldlike—bright yellows, oranges, reds
- Cockscomb—brilliant magenta
- Nube—white
- Carnations—reds, pinks
- Gladiolus—reds, oranges

SLOGANS

- The Flower(s) of the Dead
- Pathways for the Spirit(s)
- Return to the Grave
- Remembering the Dead
- A Time to Remember the Dead

- Death Is a Part of Life
- Death Is Not to Be Feared

ADDITIONAL IDEAS

Create an "ofrenda"

- Post names of deceased on bulletin board and surround with copies of flower patterns, or actual flowers
- Use graphic flower patterns. Copy any of the flower patterns and print name of deceased on flower (see **Patterns,** pp. 210–13)
- Copy any of the flower patterns onto composition paper. Students may color flowers and write poems or essays on them
- Display in combination with skeletons and skulls (see **Halloween,** pp. 24–26)

SUGGESTED USES

- Curriculum
- Seasonal
- Library/Office
- Clubs/Organizations
- Church Activities

PATTERNS
Facial Expressions

Pick the "look" that best illustrates the emotion needed.

- Happy
- Smug
- Whistling
- Sick
- Sad
- Mad

- Intelligent
- Jolly
- Delicious
- Depressed
- Worried

ADDITIONAL IDEAS

- Substitute, mix or match faces with any of our "kids."

PATTERNS
"Kids"/Head Variations

SPECIAL EFFECTS

"Kids"

- Construction paper, poster board, kraft paper, contact paper, freezer paper, oaktag

Hair

- Yarn, rope, fabric, felt, fun fur

ADDITIONAL IDEAS

- Use profiles of the "kids" with side view bodies and any of the accessories.
- Try these "kids" for an Asian look.
- Use the Indian/Mexican American maiden in combination with our Indian brave and Mexican boy.
- Sometimes a back view is very effective. Be creative!

PATTERNS
"Kids"/Multicultural

MEXICAN BOY
EAST INDIAN GIRL

SPECIAL EFFECTS

"Kids"

- Construction paper, poster board, kraft paper, wrapping paper, freezer paper, contact paper, wallpaper, oaktag, felt, fabric, fun fur

Hair

- Yarn, fabric, felt, rope, colored burlap, fun fur

ADDITIONAL IDEAS

"Kids"

- Use alone as shown, or combine with other "kids" patterns
- Hinged "kids" provide creative positioning
- For variety, use any of our "kids" or facial expression patterns
- Mix or match hairstyles and accessories

PATTERNS
"Kids"/Multicultural

ESKIMO GIRL
NATIVE AMERICAN BOY

SPECIAL EFFECTS

"Kids"

- Construction paper, poster board, kraft paper, wrapping paper, freezer paper, contact paper, wallpaper, oaktag, felt, fabric, fun fur

Hair

- Yarn, fabric, felt, rope, colored burlap, fun fur

Native American Boy

- Beads, actual feathers, leatherlike materials, ribbon, braids, trims

ADDITIONAL IDEAS

"Kids"

- Use alone as shown, or combine with other "kids" patterns
- Hinged "kids" provide creative positioning
- For variety, use any of our "kids" or facial expression patterns
- Mix or match hairstyles and accessories

ASIAN GIRL
RUSSIAN BOY

SPECIAL EFFECTS

"Kids"

- Construction paper, poster board, kraft paper, wrapping paper, freezer paper, contact paper, wallpaper, oaktag, felt, fabric, fun fur

Hair

- Yarn, fabric, felt, rope, colored burlap, fun fur

ADDITIONAL IDEAS

"Kids"

- Use alone as shown, or combine with other "kids" patterns
- Hinged "kids" provide creative positioning
- For variety, use any of our "kids" or facial expression patterns
- Mix or match hairstyles and accessories

PATTERNS
Hats—Career

- Astronaut
- Artist
- Army Helmet
- Military Cap
- Chef
- Police Officer
- Nurse
- Miner
- Firefighter
- Hard Hat

SPECIAL EFFECTS

- Construction paper, poster board, kraft paper, foamcore, felt, fabric, burlap, contact paper, leatherlike materials, clear plastic materials, ribbon, trim, rope/string

ADDITIONAL IDEAS

- All hats are sized to fit our "kids" patterns

SUGGESTED USES

- Career Day
- Curriculum
- Clubs/Organizations
- Library/Office/Cafeteria
- Church Activities

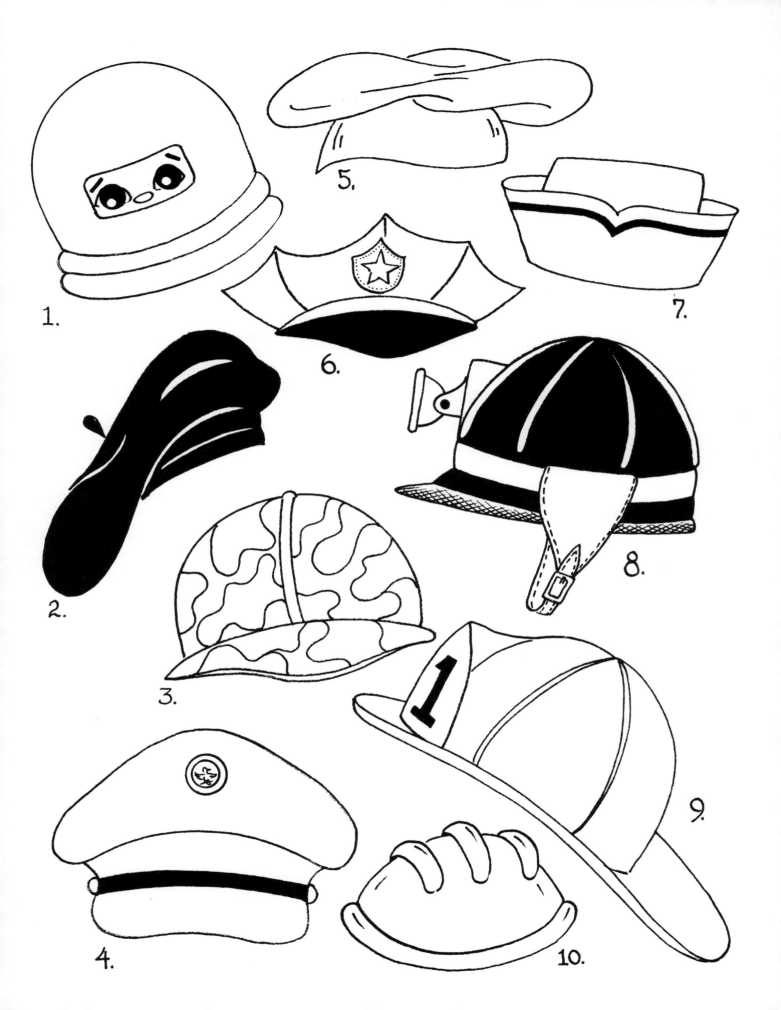

1.

2.

3.

4.

5.

6.

7.

8.

9.

10.

PATTERNS
Hats—Dress and Occasional

- Straw
- Wool
- Cowboy
- Royal/Religious
- Country Bonnet
- Sun Hat
- "Scrunch" Hat

SPECIAL EFFECTS

- Construction paper, poster board, fabric, felt, contact paper, kraft paper, foil, ribbon, trim, silk flowers, leatherlike materials

ADDITIONAL IDEAS

- All hats are sized to fit our "kids"

SUGGESTED USES

- Curriculum
- Clubs/Organizations
- Church Activities
- Western theme
- Library/Office/Cafeteria

1.

2.

3.

4.

5.

6.

7.

PATTERNS
Hats—Multicultural

- Headband/Bandanna
- Sombrero
- African Turban
- Native American Chief's Headdress
- Eastern Turban
- Asian Hat

SPECIAL EFFECTS

- Construction paper, poster board, kraft paper, foamcore, felt, fabric, burlap, contact paper, leatherlike materials, clear plastic materials, ribbon, trim, rope/string

ADDITIONAL IDEAS

- All hats are sized to fit our "kids"

1.

2.

3.

4.

5.

6.

PATTERNS
Hats—Sports

- Wrestling
- Scuba
- Football
- Baseball
- Hockey
- Skiing

SPECIAL EFFECTS

- Construction paper, poster board, kraft paper, contact paper, freezer paper, foamcore, fabric, felt, Naugahyde, foils, clear plastic materials, leatherlike materials

ADDITIONAL IDEA

- All hats are sized to fit our "kids"

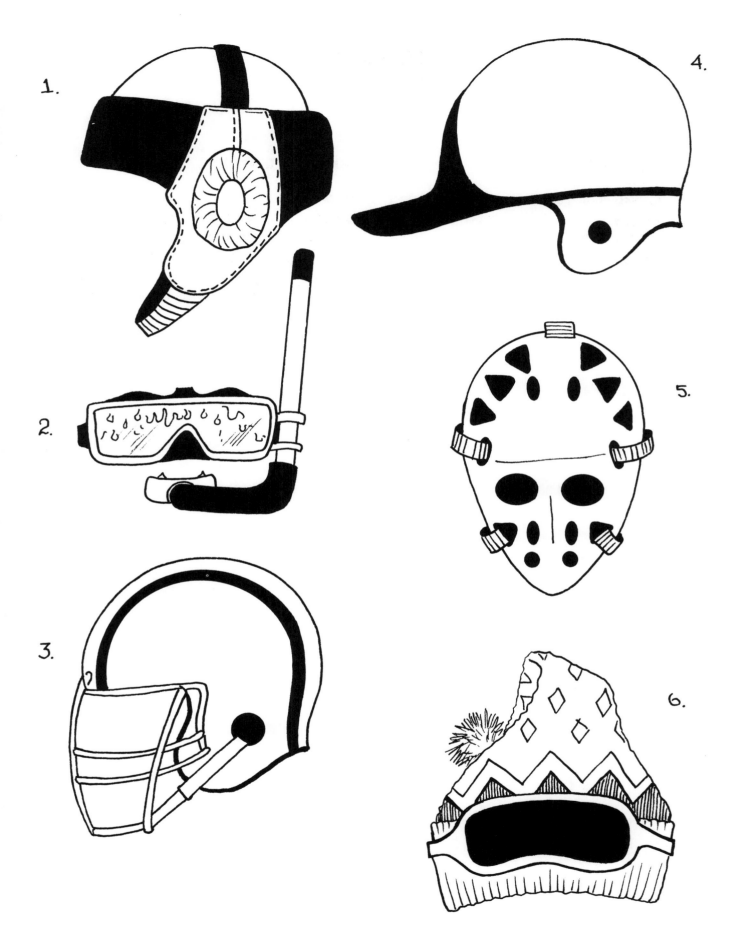

1.

2.

3.

4.

5.

6.

PATTERNS
Ghosts

SPECIAL EFFECTS

- Construction paper, white drawing paper, duplicator paper, freezer paper, contact paper, fabric, felt, plastic tablecloth, foamcore, white garbage bags, computer paper

ADDITIONAL IDEAS

Ghosts

- Use ghosts #2 and #3 around existing display areas, doors, and/or windows
- Use face and hands only as peekovers
- Make free-standing and self-supporting by using heavier materials (foamcore) and an easel
- Use on top of counters, cabinets, desks, etc.

1.

2.

3.

4.

PATTERNS
School Bus

SPECIAL EFFECTS

- Construction paper, kraft paper, poster board, freezer paper, contact paper, foam-core, yellow plastic bags

ADDITIONAL IDEAS

- Use any of our "kids" and place faces or upper bodies in windows

SUGGESTED USES

- Opening of school year
- Welcome back to school
- School Spirit Week
- Team sports and activities
- Band
- Field Trips
- Moving Up/Graduation
- Close of school year

PATTERNS
Maps

SPECIAL EFFECTS

- Construction paper, poster board, kraft paper, freezer paper, contact paper, foamcore (for the graphic map)

SUGGESTED USES

- Open House
- American Education Week
- Curriculum, especially Social Studies, Geography, Science, Current Events
- Elections
- Political Issues/Campaigns
- Fourth of July activities
- Guidance/Counselor (location of colleges and universities)

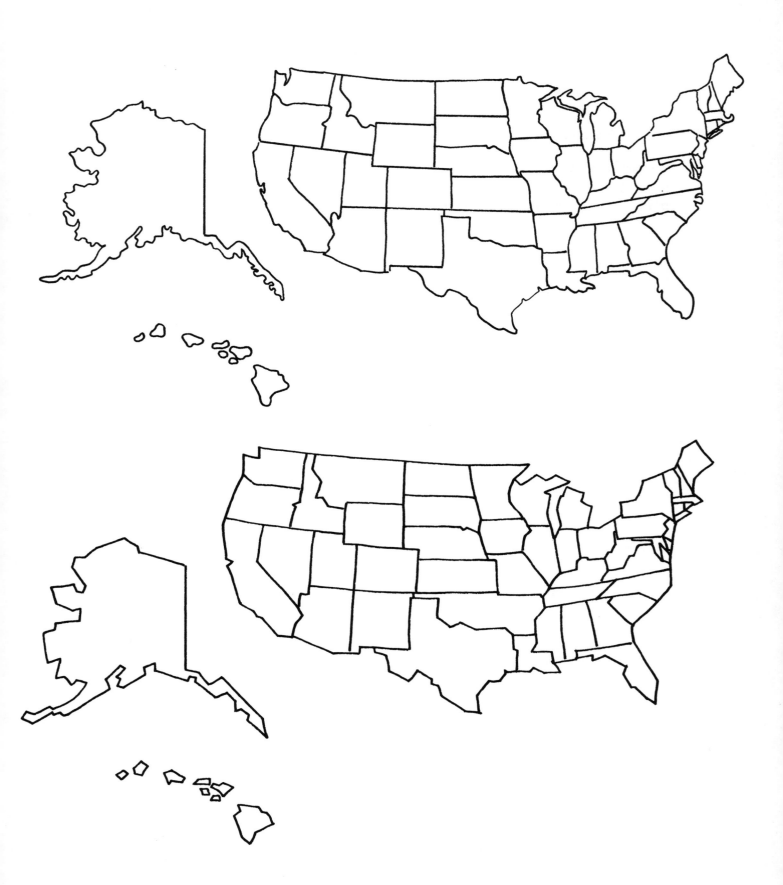

PATTERNS
Flowers—Graphic

SPECIAL EFFECTS

- Construction paper, poster board, contact paper, tissue paper, fabric, felt, wrapping paper, wallpaper, magazine covers and pages, foils, greeting cards

ADDITIONAL IDEAS

Simple flowers

- Trace around cups, bowls, saucers, any round object
- Save time by stacking and cutting four to six sheets at one time

PATTERNS
Flowers—Realistic

- Lily—represents purity, innocence, and Easter
- Iris—Greek word meaning "rainbow"
- Sunflower—represents summer and sunshine
- Rose—romance, love, friendship
- Poinsettia—tropical plant, a Christmas symbol
- Daisy—summer, freshness, youth

- Daffodil—American Cancer Society flower, represents courage and good health

SPECIAL EFFECTS

- Construction paper, poster board, kraft paper, tissue paper, freezer paper, fabric, oaktag, felt, wrapping paper, computer paper

1.

5.

4.

2.

6.

3.

7.

PATTERNS
Animals—Domestic/Farm

- Cow
- Sheep
- Mouse
- Pig
- Geese
- Dog
- Cat

SPECIAL EFFECTS

- Construction paper, poster board, kraft paper, freezer paper, fabric, felt, fun fur, cotton batting, polyester filling, plastic moving eyes, leatherlike materials, contact paper

SUGGESTED USES

- Curriculum
- Library/Office/Cafeteria
- Clubs/Organizations
- Church Activities

PATTERNS
Animals—Zoo

- Giraffe
- Seal/Sea Lion
- Camel
- Zebra

SPECIAL EFFECTS

- Construction paper, poster board, kraft paper, freezer paper, fabric, felt, fun fur, plastic moving eyes, leatherlike materials, contact paper

SUGGESTED USES

- Curriculum
- Library/Office/Cafeteria
- Clubs/Organizations
- Church Activities

PATTERNS
Animals—Zoo

- Monkey
- Lion
- Crocodile
- Elephant
- Tiger

SPECIAL EFFECTS

- Construction paper, poster board, kraft paper, freezer paper, contact paper, fabric, felt, fun fur, plastic moving eyes, leatherlike materials

SUGGESTED USES

- Curriculum
- Library/Office/Cafeteria
- Clubs/Organizations
- Church Activities
- Sports/Pep Club/Mascots

1.

4.

2.

5.

3.

LETTERING "HOW-TO'S"
Block Letters

You'll never again need stencils! Follow our directions and learn how easy it is to create your own block lettering. Customize letters to fit any size display area or space. Apply the same basic rules to all letters whether sized 2 x 4 inches or 2 x 4 feet and larger.

The alphabet shown is one example of basic block lettering where all the letters (except the I, M and W) are the same height, width, and weight (stroke thickness). The "I" is simply a single stroke while the "M" and "W" are still the same height but one stroke wider than the rest of the letters.

LETTERING "HOW-TO'S"

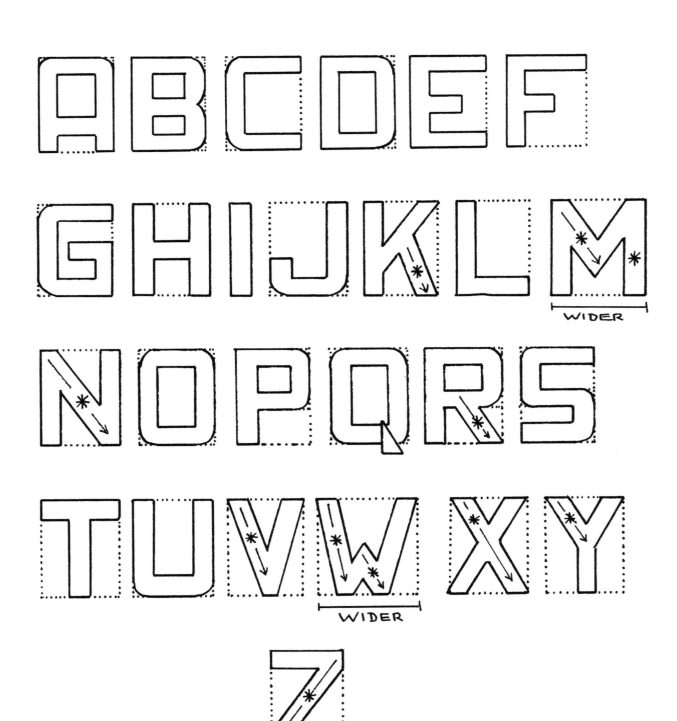

LETTERING "HOW-TO'S"
Rules

Certain rules apply to the design of a letter.

- The most common letter is one cut from a vertical rectangle where all strokes (horizontal, vertical and diagonal) are the same weight.
- A horizontal rectangle produces a short, stocky letter that can suggest power and strength. In this case the vertical stroke is much thicker than the horizontal stroke.
- Horizontal strokes can also be wider than the vertical stroke.
- Diagonal strokes, such as in the letters: K, M, N, R, V, W, X, Y, and Z should always extend out the top or bottom of the rectangle, never out the side. See rule exceptions (p. 224) if using thick and thin strokes.
- The "I" in block lettering is simply a stick that is the weight of the vertical strokes.
- The "M" and "W" are cut from rectangles that are one vertical stroke wider than the other letters.
- NOTE: The use of one thick and one thin stroke can result in interesting variations of a letter's design. Be creative but be consistent!

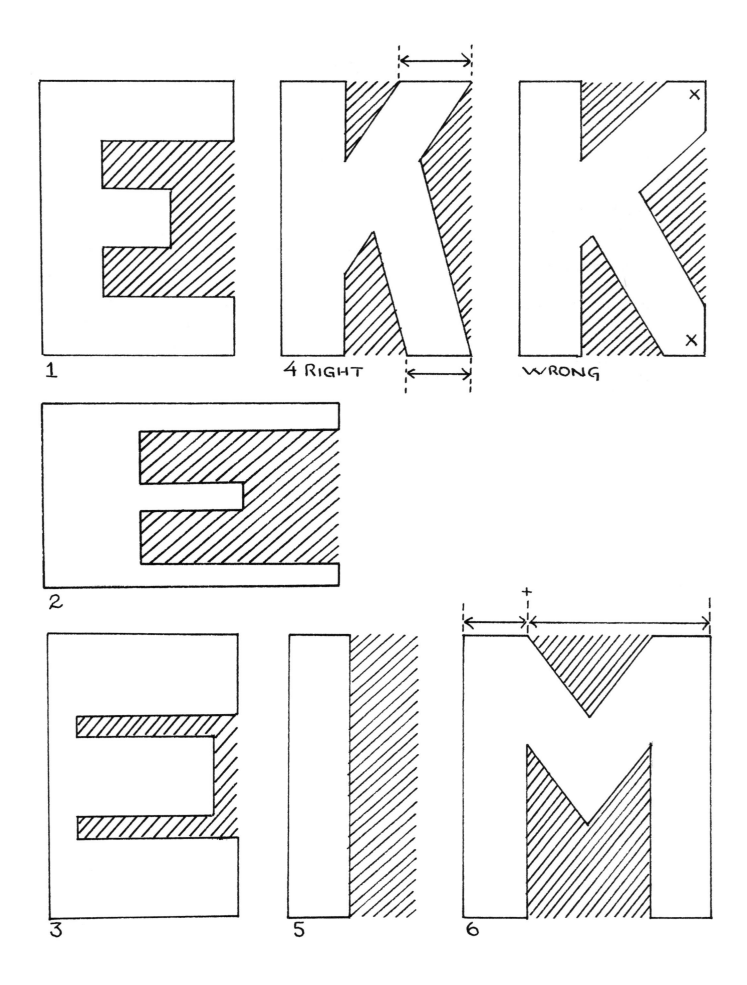

1

2

3

4 RIGHT

WRONG

5

6

LETTERING "HOW-TO'S"
Exceptions

There are variations and exceptions to the rules of cut block lettering when both thick and thin strokes are used. In this example, the vertical stroke is thick and the horizontal stroke is thin.

- Diagonal strokes slanted to the right are the thickness of the verticals. See examples: K, X, and Y.
- Exceptions to this rule are the letters M, N, and Z.
- M—This letter is cut from a rectangle that is one "thick" stroke wider. Its first vertical stroke is kept thin. Its diagonal stroke to the right is thick, and its final vertical stroke is also thick.
- N—Both vertical strokes are kept thin. Letting the diagonal to the right be the dominant thick stroke.
- Z—This letter has no vertical strokes and its only diagonal slants to the left. Keep the horizontal strokes thin and make the left diagonal thick.

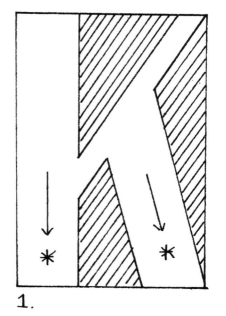
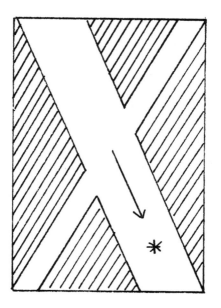
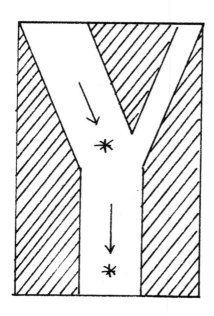

1.

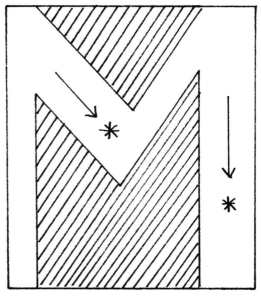
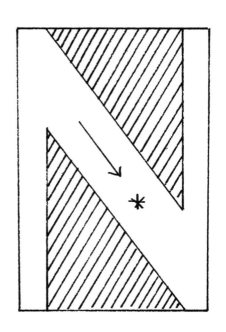
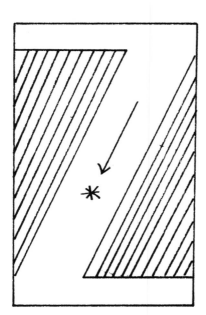

2.

LETTERING "HOW-TO'S"
Sizing

Draw a rough sketch of your bulletin board idea. Note which words are significant and size them appropriately. Count the number of letters and blanks in each line. Divide the width of your display area by this total. You now know the approximate width of each letter. The height of the letter is a matter of taste, available paper size, and space.

EXAMPLE SHOWN

Design idea reads:

We Have School
SPIRIT

- The display area is 48" wide
- There are 12 letters and 4 spaces in the first line for a total of 16 spaces
- Divide 48 by 16 = 3
- 3" is the approximate width of the letters for "We Have School"

- A standard height of 4" to 6" is appropriate for a 3" wide letter
- The word "SPIRIT" has 6 letters and the 2 spaces must be large enough for the ghosts. (total = 8 spaces)
- Divide 48 by 8 = 6
- The letters for "SPIRIT" can be 6" wide
- A standard height of 8" to 10" looks good with a 6" width
- Note: The "W" in "We" will be one stroke wider than the rest of the letters in that line. The "I"s in "SPIRIT" will simply be single strokes. This allows the word "SPIRIT" to take up less space which can then be given to the "Ghost" artwork.
- Lay out all the rectangles that have been cut for letters. If any adjustment in size is needed (trimming of width or length), do it now, before cutting the rectangles into letters.

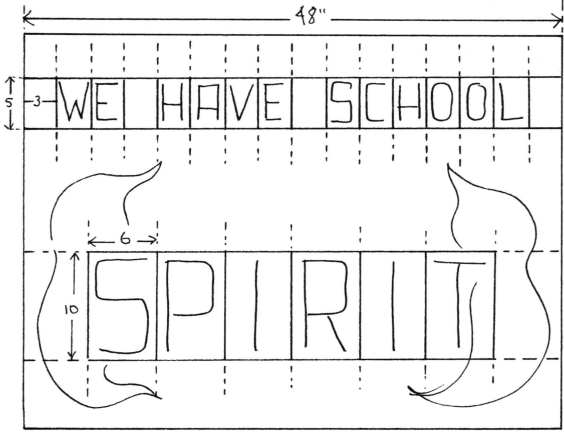

LETTERING "HOW-TO'S"
Guides

The weight or stroke of a letter is kept uniform by using a guide cut from thin but sturdy cardboard such as oaktag, folder stock or lightweight posterboard.

The size of the guide is determined by the final rectangular size of your letters. The larger the letter, the thicker and longer the guide, which is approximately one third the width of the letter.

Design variety is achieved by changing the shape or position of the rectangle and also the corresponding width of the guide.

SPECIAL EFFECTS

- Be Creative! Add flames, icicles, drips, interior textures, etc. to the cut block letters
- Substitute the straight, stick guide with a linear shape that is suited to your display theme such as: bones, logs, planks of wood, rope, etc.

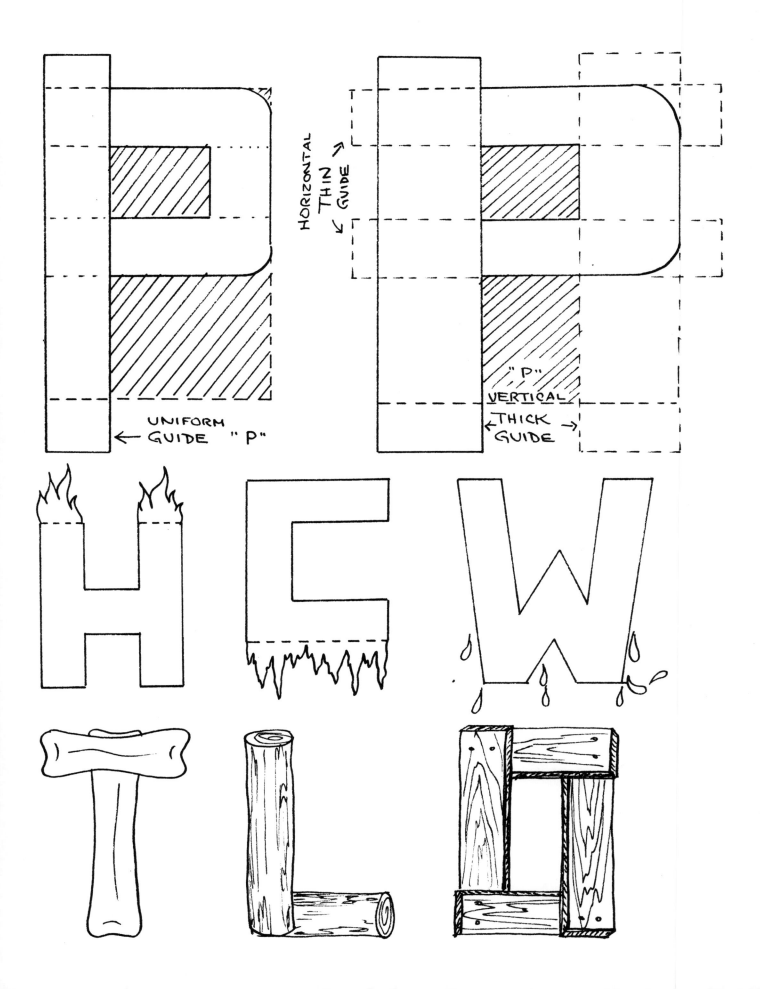

HORIZONTAL THIN GUIDE

"P" VERTICAL

UNIFORM GUIDE "P"

THICK GUIDE

GLOSSARY

Bird's Nest—Strawlike filler sold in one-pound bags.

Bolt—A lightweight fastener with a round slotted head, commonly called a stove bolt.

Collage—Three-dimensional materials applied to a flat surface.

Furring Strip—Approximately a 1" x 3" x 8′ length of pine.

Foamcore—Thin sheet of Styrofoam sandwiched between poster board. Available in various sizes, thicknesses, and colors.

Freestanding—Not attached to a wall or vertical surface. Usually supported by weight at its base.

Goop (brand name)—A strong adhesive cream cement used for bonding.

Graphic—Simplistic. Clean lines. Often geometric in design.

Luaun Plywood—A finely grained, thin, yet inexpensive plywood.

Masonite—A composite, woodlike material, finished on one side only, very strong.

Montage—A mosaic design made up of cut-and-paste papers or photographs that yields a patchwork-styled design.

Peekovers—A design cut in such a way that part of the picture appears to be peeking over the object.

Raffia—Thin strips of craft weaving that resemble straw.

Tacky Glue—A craft glue that dries clear and flexible. Especially designed for gluing odd surfaces such as wood, metal, glass, ceramics, paper, china, Styrofoam, and most plastics.

Upson Board—A heavy-ply cardboard approximately 1/8" thick.

Wet-into-wet—Painting with watercolors onto an already wet paper and allowing the colors to bleed into each other.

COMPANY RESOURCES

Many local companies generously give away their leftover materials if you ask for them. Take a chance and try it. You can save thousands of dollars for you and your organization by just calling and asking.

Publishing company
- Book covers, promotional materials for a book: banners, bumper stickers, bookmarks, posters

Paper company
- Brown kraft paper from a company that makes corrugated cardboard boxes
- White posterboard in large sheets from a company that makes white gift boxes
- Paper on a roll in a variety of colors from an envelope company

Styrofoam company
- Sheets of Styrofoam in varied thicknesses, blocks or beads of Styrofoam

Wallpaper/Paint store
- Outdated wallpaper samples, color chips, improperly mixed paint

Telephone/Electric utility company
- Colored wire, aluminum wire

Frame shop
- Foamcore, colored mat board, heavy cardboard

Print shop
- Paper

Retail stores
- Displays or posters (examples: Teddy Bear head from the Teddy Bear Graham displays, a haunted house from a Halloween candy display)
- Discount stores for sell-outs, markdowns
- Educational stores for commercial supplies
- Art stores for paper, foamcore, colored mat board

Lumber/Hardware store
- Scrap glass, Plexiglass, mirror, screening, wood; heavy cardboard tubes from linoleum

Furniture store
- Appliance boxes, heavy cardboard tubes, carpet remnants, fabric samples

Bottling company
- Rolls of colored plastic in various weights

SELECTED BIBLIOGRAPHY

Canoles, Marian L. *The Creative Copycat III*. Englewood, CO: Libraries Unlimited, 1988.

"A bulletin board is a billboard to advertise a book." Primary and secondary fiction books by 125 different authors are pictured on a one-page bulletin board.

Coplan, Kate. *Poster Ideas and Bulletin Board Techniques: For Libraries and Schools*. New York: Oceana Publications, 1981.

Through the use of simple designs and inexpensive materials, this book shows easy how-to-do-it techniques for the least experienced person. Excellent!

Fiarotta, Phyllis, and Neal Fiarotta. *Pin It, Tack It, Hang It: The Big Book of Kids' Bulletin Boards*. New York: Workman Publishing, 1975.

Illustrated in this book are 200 step-by-step instructions for constructing bulletin boards from different materials with suggestions for using them as an activity center.

Filkins, Vanessa. *Early Learning Bulletin Boards: Includes Patterns, Projects and Activities*. Carthage, IL: Good Apple, 1990.

Filkins' book includes twenty-eight seasonal and holiday bulletin boards with instructions for use in the classroom. The mobiles, borders, door and room decorations and craft projects incorporate the patterns from these bulletin boards. Excellent!

Jay, M. Ellen. *Involvement Bulletin Boards and Other Motivational Reading Activities*. Syracuse, NY: Gaylord Professional Publication, 1976.

Bulletin boards designed around a particular skill can promote the media center while incorporating contents related to the classroom program. Divided by elementary subjects, the book gives materials, procedures, student behaviors, specific examples, and unexpected outcomes.

Mallett, Jerry J. *Library Bulletin Boards and Display Kit*. West Nyack, NY: The Center of Applied Research in Education, 1984.

This book is organized in two sections—circulation motivators and skills builders, including seventy-five bulletin boards with a list of materials required, step-by-step construction, and suggested uses.

Menard, Christine. *Bright and Bold Bulletin Boards*. Hagerstown, MD: Alleyside Press, 1993.

Bulletin board ideas in this book for young adult and adult patrons include reproducible bulletin board patterns, matching bookmark designs, and instructions for making, displaying, and storing bulletin boards. Up-to-date!

Randall, Reine, and Edward C. Haines. *Bulletin Boards and Display*. Worcester, MA: Davis Publications, 1961.

Effective educational displays are shown with materials, visual tools, three dimensional displays, and lettering.

Warren, Jean. *1.2.3 Murals*. Everett, WA: Warren Publishing House, 1989.

Seasonal bulletin boards with child-centered materials are simply drawn. They are good for children's activities at a public library, day care, or Sunday school.

ABOUT THE AUTHORS

Patricia Sivak is a junior high school librarian at Greater Latrobe School District in Latrobe, Pennsylvania. She holds an undergraduate degree from Clarion State University and an M.L.S. from the University of Pittsburgh.

During her twenty-seven years as a librarian, she has supported the need for public relations in the library through bulletin boards and displays. She has written several magazine articles on this subject.

Patricia currently lives in the village of Trauger, Pennsylvania.

Mary Anne Passatore is a graduate of Edinboro University of Pennsylvania. She has been an art instructor in the Greater Latrobe School District, Latrobe, Pennsylvania, for thirty years. Currently teaching senior high art, Passatore has experience as an elementary art supervisor and a junior-high unified arts instructor.

Aside from her teaching career, Passatore is an internationally recognized "Cachet Artist" known by the name "MARICE," derived from her former name of Mary Anne Rice. She has designed and illustrated hundreds of "First Day of Issue" postal covers for GillCraft Cachets of Virginia Beach, Virginia.

She resides in Greensburg, Pennsylvania, with her husband, Jim.